Dedications:

For Robert and Sylvia Chell, Suzie Flynn, Alice Jones and Rachel Smith

In the Company of Ghosts
The Poetics of the Motorway

Edited by Alan Corkish
Co-editors: Edward Chell & Andrew Taylor

erbacce-press
Liverpool UK 2012

Copyright © 2012: erbacce-press

First edition 2012
All rights reserved

All individual photographs, essays and poems in this collection are copyright © the respective authors/photographers and cannot be reproduced without permission.

'The Autoroute and the Picturesque' by Malcolm Andrews originally appeared in *The Aesthetics of Human Environments* eds Arnold Berleant & Allen Carlson (Broadview Press, 2007); 'Looking for the Linear City' by Joe Moran originally appeared in *New Statesman*; 'In the Slipstream of Discontent' by Iain Sinclair originally appeared in *Ghost Milk* (Hamish Hamilton, 2011); 'Pile up on Levee Road' by Cralan Kelder originally appeared in *Give Some Word* (Shearsman, 2010); 'M58 Poem: Right Snow Wrong Quantities' by Andrew Taylor originally appeared in *Poetry Wales*; 'Diamond Tea' by Andrew Taylor originally appeared in *Instant Pussy*; 'Watford Gap' by Andrew Taylor originally appeared in *Comfort and Joy* (Ten Pages Press, 2011); 'Route Recalculation'

Acknowledgements:

We gratefully acknowledge the following:

The Collection of The New-York Historical Society for the photo of Central Park, TP Bennett in respect of the drawings and building designs on the rear cover (TP Bennett is the architect behind Forton Services), the photographer Sydney W. Newbery for the image on the front cover, the Yale Centre for British Art for the image of Denham Place, the National Trust for the image of Dunham Massey, Edward Chell for the photo of Darenth Interchange, Magnum for the use of Patrick Zachman's image and Alan Corkish for the image used in Angela Keaton's poem.

Cover-design and typesetting Alan Corkish.

The rights of erbacce-press to be identified as the creators
of this book have been asserted in accordance with
the Copyright, Designs and Patents Act 1988.

British Library Cataloguing-in-Publication Data
A British Library CIP record is available.

ISBN: 978-1-907878-42-8

In the Company of Ghosts
The Poetics of the Motorway

Contents:

Foreword - Edward Chell	13
M62: in the company of ghosts - John Davies	19
M58 poem: Right Snow Wrong Quantities - Andrew Taylor	27
In the Slipstream of Discontent - Iain Sinclair	29
The New M62 M57 Interchange - Hazel Mutch	37
1967 - Chris McCabe	39
'Road Race', Clio Barnard, 2005 - Elizabeth Cowie	41
Pile Up On Levee Road - Cralan Kelder	49
mr asbo - Sarah Crewe	50
The Autoroute and the Picturesque - Malcolm Andrews	53

The Road to Romance   79
- John Calvert

When A to B is not the point...   81
- David Lawrence

M56   89
- Angela Keaton

Motorway Twitter Poems   101
- Joe Moran

M62   103
- Will Alsop

Motorway Prayer Poems   107
- John Davies

Looking for the Linear City   113
- Joe Moran

Twitter poem   119
- Andrew Taylor

Soft Estate   121
- Edward Chell

Route Recalculation   129
- Andrew Taylor

A Proposal   131
- Andrew Taylor

Homes not Roads   137
- Emma Brooker

Motorway Twitter Poems 157
- Joe Moran

Diamond Tea 158
- Andrew Taylor

Extract from *Steel Girdered: A Musical in Several Parts* 160
- Jennifer Cooke

Cool Sheets + Twitter poem 162
- Andrew Taylor

Afterword: Highways and Byways 165
- Stephen Daniels

Index 169

Contributors' Biographies 173

Foreword

Motorways are not the future they are the here and the now

Motorways have been part of the British landscape for over half a century since the opening of the Preston Bypass (now part of the M6) in 1958 and the M1 the following year. Since then 2,000 miles of motorway have rolled out over the UK – a blue veined arterial system. Their ubiquitous presence informs our social and mental landscape, provides a backdrop to popular culture, and supports incrementally increasing traffic flows between our crowded conurbations. Huge distribution centres have clustered around this network shoring up and feeding our dependency on a carbon economy that will become obsolete.

The cover image of Forton Tower takes us back to the beginning, the days when 'Britain had never had it so good'. Motorways heralded an optimistic vision of progress, of transport for all. Towers, bridges and service stations, two of which have just been listed by English Heritage, define the moment when road travel captured the public imagination and motorways were full of futuristic glamour.

Forton Tower is now closed (due to asbestos), and presides like a doomed sentinel over a sclerotic M6. It resonates with the bittersweet nostalgia of a future ruin. How long before it becomes a monument to the past? The poetics of the motorway are bound up with our sense of the decline of the 'modern' as it reflects back the fallibility of our plans and dreams. Motorways are also a touchstone of the existential fragmentation that road travel engenders – a junction of many flows so self evident, functional and banal we rarely consider it. This network presents us with an unintended self-portrait, an experiential matrix; physical, cultural, political, economic, metaphoric and personal.

This book, conceived by Andrew Taylor and myself, aims to take a headlight view of these often ignored but richly modulated environments and the responses they engender. Our book intersperses work by writers, poets and artists to reveal hidden precincts of the motorway rooted in our everyday experience of the car and the motorscapes we inhabit. By giving contrasting views from the stationary, the moving, the insular and the crowd, we aim to peep inside the concrete carapace to the softer spaces within.

The book title is taken from John Davies' contribution, 'M62: in the company of ghosts'. During his motorway perambulation, Davies sensed 'a deep disconnection between drivers and their environment, themselves and those around them, themselves and their context, themselves and their own bodies'. In the kind of distorted echo this book voices, a comment posted on YouTube about the iconic 1970s Yorkie ad romanticising life on the road wryly observed 'real truckers piss in plastic bottles, shit in Tesco bags and have body odour'.

Ghosts are surprising bedfellows of the service roads and hard shoulders of our six-lane network. These arterial routes leave clues to villages buried, desire lines severed and wild places defiled. They echo to the chants and broken glasses of football coaches, road racers and un-belted joy riders, or the sighs of furtive love making in cramped Ford Escorts parked on 'dead roads'. Echoes, after-images or 'ghosts' resonate: the soft underbelly of a world so close. The contributors identify and celebrate these differing ghosts.

In the early 1990s large-scale anti-road protests led to a turning point in public attitudes towards motorways. Road protesters taking direct action against the M3 extension at Twyford Down brought environmental concerns firmly into the public arena. While the protest failed to stop the road, the Conservative government's 'Roads for Prosperity' program, adopted by Margaret Thatcher in the 1980s in what she described as 'this great car economy', was finally dropped by the incoming Labour government in 1997.

While the freeway is a trope at the heart of American culture, the

British motorway is a more subdued sibling; less epic, more dowdy, with its own peculiarly subversive enchantments. J.G. Ballard explored this hinterland in books such as *Crash* and *The Concrete Island*, as have more recently Iain Sinclair with *London Orbital* and Joe Moran with *On Roads*. A growing interest in these peripheral and threshold worlds is further illustrated by the recent non-fiction *Edgelands: Journeys into England's True Wilderness* by poets Paul Farley and Michael Symmons-Roberts. Writers such as Marc Augé or Julio Cortázar and Carol Dunlop have described the 'non-places' around the motorways of Europe. Our book seeks to complement texts like these. We have taken an interdisciplinary approach; however this book is not a survey but a starting point: an attempt to focus our readers' attention on the rich and surprising diversity of our encounters on and with the motorway.

We would point readers towards new responses that we do not have space to include. Graphic designer Mike Webb has created a minimal publication revealing a bird's eye view of the motorway junctions of the M6 (one of which we reproduce here; p90). Celebrating the fortieth anniversary of the Gravely Interchange, also known as Spaghetti Junction, artist Graeme Miller made his piece 'Track'. Participants would glide along rails running under the interchange while lying on their back, undergoing 'a solitary, immersive experience as the landscape is transformed around them'. Other more secretive urban explorers investigate the grander architecture of motorway infrastructure, such as the Thelwall Viaduct which takes the M6 over the Manchester Ship Canal presenting enigmatic on-line photographic postings of the interior.

Fifty years ago, motorways were strangely denuded places with verges like snooker table baize. It is only more recently that vegetation has sprung up and then been managed, landscaped and designed to keep cars in and sound out. Already this landscaping of larger roads has within it the seeds of possible future 'greenways' where the asphalt soft-top might be penetrated by the rock drill of Japanese knotweed and colonized by other more native species. Our road system could in the future be like the Nazca lines of Peru. Some already argue that the future of mass transport lies in rail. The old British Rail slogan 'We're getting there' now sounds more like a forewarning.

Motorways have ploughed through the landscape, changed the way it looks and changed the way we look at and experience our surroundings – through the car windscreen at speed. This book encourages us to Stop, Look and Listen to the unnoticed worlds in this territory.

Edward Chell

M62: in the company of ghosts

I walked home, from Hull to Liverpool, following the route of the M62. Staying within earshot of the carriageways through the motorway's rural sections; wandering off-line to spend days in the towns and cities en-route. Seeking local company, to hear stories of life on that road. Two months of deliberately slow travelling, through an unusually mild autumn. All the way, I found myself in the company of ghosts.

At dusk on the day I reached the end of the M62 (The Rocket Interchange, Broadgreen, Liverpool), not far away two boys, Kieran (7) and Guy (6) attempted a short-cut home by riding their toy scooters across the M56 motorway in Preston Brook, Runcorn. In the growing dark they were unsighted until close up. The drivers of three vehicles hastening home at the end of the rush hour could not avoid hitting them. The boys died instantly. As for the adults involved – drivers, parents, neighbours who had spoken to the boys minutes before – something terrible was awakened in them by this awful incident. In their troubled TV interviews, you could see it in their eyes.

All along my two-month journey I had seemed to be sensing ghosts. Absences in the presence. Presences in the absence. I gazed out from Hornsea in awareness of the ancient villages of Holderness lost to the brutal North Sea: calm waters overlying Waxholme, Colden Parva, Hrafnseyrr, and all the other almost forgotten villages which slipped into the sea centuries ago; oil tankers from the Humber Refinery riding the waves fathoms above the drowned ruins of Ravenser Odd, 'an extremely famous borough' (according to the Chronicle of Meaux Abbey) before its inundation in 1360.

I became fascinated by the numerous 'dead roads' en-route: once vibrant highways or viable country lanes which were sundered by the building of the motorway and its service routes, and which now through society's inattention and unconcern have been reborn as neglected wildlife havens, dumping sites, and secluded positions for clandestine afternoon liaisons (couples clinched in one of two vehicles parked together). At Junction 23 below Outlane, the M62's noise and the disruption in the air perpetuate the violence of the motorway's construction. For Outlane is a viciously severed village. Alongside the bridge across the junction, a row of houses directly abut the carriageways' edge, rising high above the road. This is at Leeches Hill on New Hey Road, a long road out of Huddersfield which is re-routed through the motorway roundabout, but whose original course on each side of the motorway shows the village of Outlane with its nerve ends exposed to the M62. Six carriageways fire traffic ferociously through what used to be the village high street. I found myself following the imagined line of the demolished houses through the air in the chasm above the motorway, connecting the old road back to itself, sensing a place which is no longer there.

The M62 makes spectral sounds, under the M62 Ouse Bridge: where in a wide, dusty agricultural plain under a high sun a few steps into the bridge's shadow remove all vehicular movements from view, and in the sudden stillness the senses open to the booming, cracking, clanking, noises above. The steel plate girders in the bridge's body rattle like prisoners in chains as countless juggernauts batter over them, wheels whistling and tyres thudding over the reinforced concrete deck slabs. In a narrow lane of trees between IKEA and the M62, Birstall, and on cobblestoned Philips Park Road alongside the hidden motorway near Whitefield, similarly hissing, slashing, whispering spectres accompanied me on my way. Standing north west of Scammonden Reservoir, by a fence bordering the eastbound edge of the motorway Brian, a local farmer, raised his voice above the roaring traffic to tell me that the scattered stones by which we stood were, until the coming of the M62, a hamlet called Han Head. The two brothers who farmed each side of the valley were both loud characters, and regularly held conversations with each other across the open space. Their sister never left Han Head in her life – 'except to be buried', Brian said. And while he told me this, an unending flow of travellers flashed past us. In the minute it took him to relay this tale probably a few hundred vehicles had passed us by. The drivers' lives-in-motion and that woman's so-static existence, the deafening engine screams and the brothers' valley-wide discourses: all were alive to me in that moment.

I made my walk a coast-to-coast journey, Hornsea to Crosby, as the M62 begins and ends rather anonymously (alongside agricultural sheds near North Cave, west of Hull, where the A63 melts away into the motorway, and in the ten-lane concrete intrusion into suburban Liverpool at Broadgreen). It was on the thirteenth night of my journey, my fourth night on the M62, that I had the most vivid otherworldly encounter of the trip. Restless in bed, due to the undoubted thrill of having reached Goole, and perhaps more immediately to the high temperature of my rooftop room in the Clifton Hotel and Chinese Restaurant on busy Boothferry Road, in the midnight dark I opened my eyes, frustrated from my futile attempts to slumber, and sat upright as facing me in a sepia glow on the opposite wall, was an apparition. The shape of a cloaked person, with a thin head or perhaps wearing some sort of crown – like one of the *Magi* – looked down on me. Formed on the wall by streetlight diffusing through net curtains this still, nocturnal visitor seemed to me a calming presence. Not the shape of those fevered ghosts I'd encountered underneath the Ouse Bridge, this was more a quietly welcoming spirit. In my state of altered consciousness it didn't take me long to decide who this kindly visitor was. I gave this shape a name: The Goodly Spirit of Goole. I sought out his gentle presence as I explored the town the following day, and concluded that he could be Cornelius Vermuyden, the man celebrated as the founder of the modern port of Goole, 1630s constructor of the Dutch River, which drained the marshland and opened up valuable trade routes. His presence was everywhere thereabouts.

At Boggart Hole Clough in North Manchester, Phil Smith and I walked in search of boggarts, which are sprites, mischievous spirits mainly found in Lancashire and Yorkshire, often thought to be responsible for poltergeist activity and pranks like turning the doorstep milk sour, making things disappear and causing dogs to go lame. They live in mossy places, and north-east Manchester has many mossy places, among them the spooky Clough, mist-shrouded on that October morning. The spirit we actually encountered on the walk was of another sort altogether. It was the spirit of Emmeline Pankhurst, Mancunian suffragette, who, we discovered, had addressed crowds of 25,000 to 40,000 at Boggart Hole Clough in May 1896, and was summonsed and charged with breaching public order. Here was mischief of another order, in the park where Pankhurst and her comrades strove to awaken the public to issues of equality and democracy, and where reportedly she caught a bad cold from so much standing around speaking. As we wandered through Boggart Hole Clough our feet trod the very ground where the tactics of the suffragette struggle had been honed: gaining maximum publicity by refusing to accept legal judgements; this was the place where Emmeline Pankhurst's star first rose as she pushed herself on to the stage of national politics on her own terms rather than in support of her husband. Boggart Hole Clough: indeed, a place of history-making mischief.

Other presences informed my walk. Crab Man Phil Smith, whose collaborators in the *Mis-Guide* projects gave me strategies for roaming urban spaces (for instance, walking a sign of the cross through central Leeds to see what was at its heart. It turned out to be a leisure centre called The Light). London Orbiter Iain Sinclair, who said of his M25 project that the whole point was to walk the motorway spaces, and thereby 'to suck out information slowly and gradually from the ground'. Deep topographer Nick Papadimitriou, aka *The London Perambulator*, who has cultivated the habit of 'looking through the gaps between suburban houses, to gain a glimpse of old oak or ash trees growing somewhere further off, in back gardens or on the Green Belt', and to permit these giants 'to remind us that, interpenetrating the electrically lit safety of our double-glazed homes and the ruthless quest for utility manifest in our concretised front gardens, there is an older world which will not go away, a realm whose concerns are not those of the human one'. Charles Hurst, whose *Book of the English Oak* describes his epic 1909 walk, planting acorns all the way from Manchester to the

East Midlands, and whose philosophy, 'the gentle art of strolling', involved the practice of walking 'a good English mile in an hour'. The M62 is 105 miles long. Mimicking Hurst, I took two months to walk it. That averages at 1.7 miles per day.

The M62 ends at a railway junction, Broadgreen Station, and the pub across the flyover from there is called The Rocket. It invokes the ghost of William Huskisson MP who was killed by the train of that name at the Rainhill Trials in 1829. As Rebecca Solnit points out in *Wanderlust*, Huskisson was not mourned by the crowd then or remembered by anyone since, our heads having been turned by the speed of the motorised vehicle. And all along my route, on motorway bridges and beside every other form of roadway I saw floral tributes tied to trees and lamp posts, memorialising those who died just there at their or someone else's wheel, and whose spirits hover in horror and condemnation, while the traffic speeds on past.

Influenced by the moving images in Chris Petit's *London Orbital* film, his camera mounted on M25 bridges, pointing into the car space of unaware drivers, their faces appearing *Skrik*-like on the screen, I stood most days on platforms above the M62 overlooking hundreds of vehicles rocketing beneath, the deranging violence of their motion rocking the bridge stanchions, exposing my sense of vulnerability. I saw the fixed look on the drivers faces, the greyness in their eyes and the whiteness of their wheel-grasping hands, and I repeatedly heard a voice from Eliot come to me, describing this eidolonic scene: *I had not thought death had undone so many.* The death I was sensing was a deep disconnection between drivers and their environment, themselves and those around them, themselves and their context, themselves and their own bodies. That's why I decided to walk the M62. To do it more slowly, to feel it on foot, to breathe it more closely, to embrace the territory. It was only later, influenced by Tim Edensor's paper *M6 Junction 19-16: Defamiliarizing the Mundane Roadscape*, that I came to recognise that 'both homely familiarities and imaginative connections can be fostered' in the 'mundane space-time' of the speeding vehicle.

At Junction 24 at Ainley Top, and on Windy Hill near Saddleworth Moor, the high places of the route where the redundant chimneys and reclaimed chapels of Rochdale and Halifax sprawl within vast moors, I found myself reimagining Roman Legions moving across the landscape of the North. This must have been a frightening vision in its day: one to send you scurrying to safety, deeply fearful of the deathly power in those booted feet. And on those hilltops another M62 vision was born: of a day – not in my day but perhaps in a day which the classmates of Kieran and Guy will see – when the motorways will become dead roads, mossed over, and people will walk them, fantasising about the violent roaring vehicle convoys which once used them. After the oil runs out, or some inevitable catastrophe hits our dying civilisation, future people will look back on us that way. We will be ghosts to them.

John Davies

M58 poem: Right Snow Wrong Quantities

There is salt despite being
nowhere near   the sea
it sprays from surface
to screen   we seek the north

and recreation

the hills a white tint legacy
of location   spots of time
the nourishment   of minds

repaired invisibly

such sound   landscape matched
sonic cathedrals   made out of ice

Love is undefined   it enters the hall
cloaks itself amongst antiquities
            amongst the views to the lake
along the stalled grass to the shore

it is looped in piano music in refrains
in dimly lit buildings   snow gathered

against dry stone walls   it is here

the air is different
reminiscent of Europe   cloudless
stars   clearer

like gathered polished stones initialled

Snow is in the air
         despite forecast
whispering in   naked hedgerows

it arrives   upon departure

Andrew Taylor

In the Slipstream of Discontent

The Will Alsop project that concerned me now was his take on the coast-to-coast motorway, Hull to Liverpool, the M62. Hungry for a larger canvas than Barnsley, the architect proposed a SuperCity folded around the entire road. He published an illustrated book of supporting essays. And he promoted the idea, vigorously, with a television film. As a presence admitted to the intimacy of our screens, Alsop looks like a man who gives (and receives) good lunch; excellent company, reflex cigarette. Easy shirt, unstructured French-blue artisan's jacket. Freeflowing monologues in a seductive deepthroat growl. Projects collapse, prizes are won. There is commissioned work in Germany and in France. And lottery-funded crumbs in the English badlands, marginal constituencies unlucky enough to be noticed by box-ticking central government. A topography of virtual masterpieces that will never be built. Noughties architecture is the art of getting some other sucker to take the blame.

Discovered, nozzling his jeep on a northern forecourt, Alsop can't wait to grab a felt-tipped pen and deface the windscreen. He lights up, before taking stock of his surroundings: 'Cheap and nasty. Horrid, revolting, evil. Complete and utter shit'. Here is a motorway utopian, an architect accepting just enough work to fund his true passion, painting. Painting on windows. Cartoons teased from agribiz edgelands. Coloured pens rattle across the dashboard. Tobacco contrails improve the visual complexity. Thick gold signet ring on paw. An actor who can drive and talk at the same time. Man of the road. Service-station philosopher.

He strikes east out of Liverpool, making for the M62, heading for Hull and memories of childhood. He schmoozes the fixed camera, architecture as infotainment. 'It's about playing.' He gestures towards a ravished horizon of cooling towers, no-purpose sheds and glinting rivers. 'This is an itinerant area that you can't define as country or city.' There is nothing quite so agreeable as pulling onto the hard shoulder, to conjure, pen on glass, soft-sculptures from innocent ground which would otherwise be polluted by Barratt estates. Chris Petit, when we motored up and down the boulevards of Alsop's imaginary city, admitted that, on the whole, he'd rather take up residence in a skip alongside a smoking landfill mountain on Rainham Marshes.

Alsop needs a bed for the night. What can the road offer? Patrick Keiller, reprising Daniel Defoe's *Tour through the Whole Island of Great Britain*, for his film *Robinson in Space*, speaks with weary affection of the Travelodge franchise. You know exactly what you are going to get: minimalism. Minimal efficiency, minimal fuss, minimal satisfaction. The budget hotel, the overnight stay on expenses, is a salient feature of the SuperCity. Alsop describes the experience in terms of Chaucerian collisions.

'People don't actually meet or talk in hotels,' he told me, when I visited him at the offices of his architectural practice, in a leafy and salubrious riverside quarter of London. 'If you go to a hotel chain, it's perfectly clean and comfortable, but the public spaces aren't there. You're not expected to sit around and mingle. They're missing a trick. All these guys, particularly travelling salesmen, have a lot of stories. Hotels are not creating the stage for things to happen.'

In SuperCity, social interaction is important; partying, yarning at leisure over good food. That classic exchange between travellers, pilgrims with experiences to share. Dimly-lit bars from which consenting adults walk away unscathed. One-night stands of reps, evangelists, tribute bands, traded footballers, academics without tenure, oil-company hatchetmen deciding where they can close another filling station. Neon nests where transients, coming off-road with the glamour of elsewhere, make a pitch to the girl behind the counter. The nightscape of the American Depression as reflected in film noir dreams. *Fallen Angel. Out of the Past (*aka *Build My Gallows High). They Drive by Night. The Postman Always Rings Twice.*

With the shudder of traffic still in the vein, the hard miles between Burnley, Bradford, Pontefract, Alsop made a big decision: *they are all the same.* A specialist cheese counter, a theatre forty miles to the south, a night on the town: parochial divisions no longer play.

'If these people live in Barnsley and they want an upmarket shop, they go to Leeds. If they want a jolly good market – they used to have one of their own, but it's gone – they drive to Doncaster. If they feel like a good thrash in the evening, they think nothing of heading off to Manchester. They use this plethora of towns, cities and villages, as one SuperCity. All I had to do was stretch the concept to take in Liverpool and Hull.'

Framed in the sunset window of his vehicle, this prophet of centralism is a true icon. The hieratic representation of a sacred personage lasered into glass. Adrift on the M62, meditating on the death of locality, Alsop is as much a representative of his period as Vincent Van Gogh in that molten self-portrait, *Painter on the road to Tarascon*.

'If you take roughly twenty miles on either side of the M62, there are roughly 15.4 million people. Your journey can take forever, because of the traffic. Or it can be clear and quick. That's how I came to the conclusion that it would be a very good thing to *increase* the density. All those towns and cities are charged with building more houses. What they do, all the housing providers like Wimpey and Barratt, they look at the cheap option – which is to build on the edge of existent centres. This is not good practice. There are lots of places in the middle of those cities where you can build. There is no shortage of derelict sites. There are vast tracts of car parks just waiting.'

The M62 induces reverie, Wordsworthian recollections of childhood. Alsop grew up in Northampton. There is a moment in his television documentary when he speaks about standing on a motorway bridge with his father, gazing down on the traffic, road as river, before a family picnic in an adjacent field. His father died within a week of this epiphany.

Hull, the architect reported, was the destination for a holiday with a friend whose father was in the wet fish trade. 'It was thriving, a real fishing port. On the other side of the river, they took all the elements of the catch, crushed at the bottom of the hold, and turned them into pet food. The whole port was full of women in pinnies gutting fish. All these people lived in terraced houses which backed on to the river.'

Alsop spoke of Mr Bogg, an employer on the docks. 'They're buggers in Hull,' this man said. 'They steal my wooden fish boxes to make furniture. I wouldn't mind, but whenever they go anywhere the sods ride in a taxi.'

Determined to test the Alsop thesis, I took to the road with the film essayist Chris Petit. Raw from a sleepless Hull night, punctuated by screams, smashed glass, slammed doors, Chris discovered that his silver Merc, secure in the hotel's basement garage, had been the venue for an unauthorised party. Night staff didn't waste the opportunity to entertain in a motor of that vintage, in such leathery comfort. After cleaning out the kebab wraps and knotted condoms, and winding down the electric windows, we headed for the M62. Pausing only to pay tribute to John Prescott's favourite trough, Mr Chu's China Palace riverside restaurant. A lion-guarded, green and red stockade: like the set for Nicholas Ray's epic, *55 Days at Peking*. I told Chris that I couldn't accept Will Alsop's contention, one of the articles of faith around which his SuperCity thesis was developed.

'It struck me,' Alsop said, 'that if Leeds and their football team fell out of the FA Cup, the natural thing would be for the supporters to cheer Manchester United or Manchester City. Then you have a regional identity, one city.'

About as natural, I thought, as incest. And much less popular. Leeds and Manchester United as companions in arms? Jack Charlton and 'our kid' sharing a damp Woodbine in the bath? Happy-go-lucky Billy Bremner tickling the ribs of Nobby Stiles? Trans-Pennine blood feuds are often a matter of a few hundred yards of disputed ground. If there is anything that unites the whole SuperCity, it's the quality of hatred: Liverpool-Manchester-Leeds. Badge-kissers, coin-throwers, karate-kickers: united in the obscenity of their tribal chants.

Michael Moorcock spent several years in a rambling house at Ingleton, close to the Yorkshire/Lancashire border. 'No question that the Wars of the Roses lived on,' he told me. 'The towns around Leeds all had very strong identities and a sense of superiority one to another. My friend Dave Britton says that although everything has changed on the surface in Manchester, with new council estates replacing terraces, the basic character remains the same. Markets where markets always were, violence where violence always was. The notion of supporting Leeds had him laughing like Bernard Manning.'

The M62, Petit reckoned, along that first stretch out of Hull, was almost as good as East Germany, the run he'd made from Berlin to the Baltic. Our transit was silk-smooth, traffic light. The cooling stacks at Selby are always worth a photo or two. We pulled off-highway at Saddleworth Moor, to take in, from this rugged tump, the hazy spread of Manchester. Once again dark history infected our perceptions. You are never free of that hideous back story, the abused and buried children. The ones who have never been recovered. And the malignant urban picnickers with their leaking newspaper faces: bottles of cheap wine, tartan rug and spade. The satanic version of *Coronation Street* spoiling the ground even now. The thing they murdered was the moor itself.

Step outside the car and everything changes. Wind cuts. A road sign for Saddleworth has the Oldham part of it peeled away like a second-degree burn, a failed graft. Limestone overwhelmed by Millstone Grit. A rough track leading to the Pennine Way. Low cloud, saturated air. Rubbish pits and tyre dumps in which unwanted things cook and sulk. Mesh fence protecting pylons barnacled with humming disks, eavesdropping equipment. Cars that stop here are suspect, furtive; out of place until the rubber rots from the wheels and they sink into the peat.

Coming the other way, east, as part of his television tour, Will Alsop pulled in for a comfort break. 'What Saddleworth Moor needs,' he said, 'is more access roads and a fancy service station.' He clambers from his high chariot, yawns and scratches. 'Let's make a beautiful rural service area at this point. With fantastic food and unbelievable shops.' A 24-hour destination magnet appealing to the nightbirds of SuperCity. And who would they be? Entertainers, reps. Haunted solitaries. The feral underclass populating crime encyclopaedias. Gloved wheelmen in white company vans cruising a connected network of red light districts. Tabloid monsters with claw-hammers and faulty moral wiring. Film-makers stitching swans' wings on corpses.

* * *

We looped Manchester, looped everywhere. When it works, and you float through the cinema of landscape, nobody wants to come away from the road. We'd visited Liverpool a few months earlier, to shoot a piece for the Audi Channel, driving a £60,000 luxury model from the Antony Gormley beach at Crosby into North Wales; now Petit suggested a detour to Morecambe. A detour which involved a truckstop at Carnforth that demonstrated the qualities a pop-up city should possess: efficient but unobtrusive service based around clean and functional architecture, American windows on English lethargy. Comfortable chairs, hot soup, and a silent television screen running Euro-junk football as an analgesic, a meditative panel with no emotion, no content. Electronic impressionism: lush greens, patterns forming and reforming as colour-coordinated athletes drift and sway. You can eat here, sleep here, shop here – and, best of all, park without hassle. The lorry park *is* a park, enclosed, muffled, with great shining transcontinental rigs as works of sculpture. In the approved SuperCity fashion, this refuge has no allegiance to the local; to Carnforth with its stagnant bookshop and its heritaged railway station, the self-denying ghosts of *Brief Encounter*. The truckstop was: Belgium, Italy, Idaho, Oregon. In a cartography of absence, here at last was an oasis of the possible that required no intervention from planners or overexcited architects.

Morecambe, half-resuscitated, half-choked on the karma of the drowned Chinese cockle pickers, was an unresolved argument between entropy and aspiration. With a grand sweep of bay for which the inhabitants seemed to have no particular relish. A woman, out early, dragging a blind German shepherd dog, chatted with a street cleaner in a yellow tabard. 'He's moulting, luv. It's fab. Like getting new carpet for front room.'

Iain Sinclair *Extracted from* GHOST MILK.

The New M62 M57 Interchange

There   I was alone in the night   suddenly
                                                  curving
            in a camber of shellgrip

Here   I imagine
                    I skim
the image
              along a smooth dune   and long for
                            the whole movement

There   were ragas
in dark blue ripples from a CD to my skull
                                            (a shell)

Now   a black sky backdrift is leaking
a tanpura drone   in ascending pitch
                             surging with the rise

I saw a planet   that night
      pierce the yellow scorch

one halogen note still remains   quavering
                                 on the arc of a dark
                                 chord   pressed in
                                          white space

     Hazel Mutch

1967

Less than a grub specked in the engine's womb
less than a lock picked by the wind
less than fame – money – love
less than woodlouse
less than Rimbaud
less than health
less than gravel
less than dole
less that truth

A Bash Street Kids bouffant splits ends in a craw of consonants
a moment of no blue plaque on Charing X Road
MACSWEENEY WAS HERE
before the undertaker flanked in Soviet black
hair grey as hoarfrost bled by forged passports
took you away from the glare of your audience
in the back of a car, destination Cambridge
– via Holborn, Euston, Hampstead –
a mass crowd of stars swerving into side-doors
a dog-rug, ashtray, manual handle
– the stars numerous as the fizz of alcohol –
the back of the undertaker's head transfixed
bigger than Johnny Cash, Chatterton, Dylan
his steady silent hands tapping out more than words
that motorways are just dictionaries with space inside
– CAMBRIDGE 59 MILES –
adrenalin spooring your blood's comet-tails
too drunk to guess   all motorways fork   in silence

[Barry MacSweeney was 'spotted' by JH Prynne at his first London reading on Charing X Road and apparently driven by Prynne back to Cambridge that night]

Chris McCabe

'Road Race', Clio Barnard, 2005

M_y_ _i_d_e_a_ _o_f_ _a_ _p_i_e_c_e_ _o_f_ _s_c_u_l_p_t_ u_r_e_ _i_s_ _a_ _r_o_a_d_._ _T_h_a_t_ _i_s_,_ _a_ _r_o_ a_d_ _d_o_e_s_n_'t_ _r_e_v_e_a_l_ _i_t_s_e_l_f_ _a_t_ _a_ n_y_ _p_a_r_t_i_c_u_l_a_r_ _p_o_i_n_t_ _o_r_ _f_r_o_m_ _a_n_y_ _p_a_r_t_i_c_u_l_a_r_ _p_o_i_n_t_. Carl Andre.[1]

_ Andre's analogy of road and sculpture strikes me as a particularly rich way to think about Clio Barnard's *Road Race*, a two-screen gallery installation work, for Andre introduces temporality in invoking the idea of the continuousness of a road that cannot be known at or from any particular point. The sculptural object in its three-dimensionality exists as a continuous surface and form that is experienced differently from each and any of the multiple places of view it engages. It cannot be taken in at a single glance, requiring an embodied relation as the spectator moves around the work, as well as a temporal process of remembering. The time-based work's two-dimensionality can become sculptural when the screen itself becomes an object in space, and what is seen and heard is engaged spatially and no longer from a single position, in contrast the cinema seat's fixed place of viewing.[2] *Road Race* engages us as sculptural not only because it requires us to engage in a bodily movement of viewing its two channels of information – one a video monitor, the other a large wide-screen cinema-format projection – but also because it requires of us a process of recollection and re-assembly in relation to the repetitions and differences of the roads and races we watch, and the stories of documentary and fiction it presents.

A road takes one somewhere, it connects spaces and places and it constitutes a theatre of movement as traversal in a crossing of space. Motorways do it faster, but less poetically. We take a road to go somewhere, but roads themselves also take us – metaphorically – on journeys, such as Orwell's exploration of the bleak living conditions of the working classes in Lancashire and Yorkshire in *The Road to Wigan Pier* (1937), or the road to health, or to enlightenment, whether

Saint Paul on the road to Damascus, or more pedestrian knowledge.

The motorway does not seem to have lent itself to metaphor as easily, it is somehow too literal and descriptive, instead it is subject to metaphor, for example the M1 was called 'the artery of Britain', as an image of connectivity, dynamic and life-giving, but also pumping the nation with goods. Motorways are exclusive – forbidding pedestrians, cyclists, and horses for example. And they regulate, for whatever the term – autobahn autoroute, freeway, expressway, etc – they are exclusively for high-speed vehicular traffic, with traffic flow and ingress/egress organised to provide unhindered, continuous movement. Slip roads allow escape to other routes and to motorway rest stops that each involve a navigational challenge. Motorways have hard shoulders for emergency use only, in contrast to the pavements or soft verges of roads that can be used by everyone (except, of course privately owned ones). But beyond the hard shoulder is a verdant in-between world, which for Edward Chell is a powerful visual metaphor that 'signifies on the one hand the power of the state to order, monitor, control and restrict access and on the other hand, the complex frothing patterns of the flowers and vegetation seem like a kind of scurrilous rococo flourish of uncontrollable nature – freedom.' (http://www.edwardchell.com/ten-steps-to-heaven-text/) It is as a space, rather than as a conduit, that the motorway can become figural.

In *Road Race*, the motorway is the ground and figure for a formal, aesthetic, exploration of the cinematic, as moving images and sounds, juxtaposed with a documentary heard and seen of recorded interviews. The controlled space of the motorway is challenged by the travellers who organise races that are run at dawn on motorways and roads in Britain. It is a collective but secretive activity performed in a public space, involving a group of spectators who form a rolling road-block with their cars while two trotting horses, with sulkies (two-wheel carriages) and drivers, run a very fast race on the motorway. The racing is a misuse of the motorway, not only illegally blocking it, but also diverting its purpose, of enabling journeying to somewhere fast by *motor* vehicle, and instead competing to arrive at a fixed point by horse drawn carriage.

In the gallery installation for *Road Race*'s two screens, a television monitor is placed to the side and in front of a cinematic widescreen back projection; each shows a loop of six sequences, whose appearance on screen, and their alternation, are carefully synched. The monitor presents in series three interviews with different travellers, each framed by black leader, and each followed by the same shots of a race at dawn (when they are always held) and recorded in hand-held digital video, 'vérité' style, from within a car; this series is then repeated. On the cinema screen a filmed race is also seen, but it is shot on super-16mm from several camera positions in front and beside the horses, and the following cars; this race however is a reenactment that is carefully staged and timed for the cameras (filmed over the course of a sunny winter's day and graded to look as though it is dawn). We see this re-enactment in six versions, each with a different editing of sound and image that variously foregrounds dialogue from the 16mm shoot, or from the digital video shoot, or uses voice-over from the interviews, or overlaid ambient noises of the cars, the horses hooves, bird songs. One version is heard with a full post-produced music scoring as well as sounds and dialogue, heard in surround-sound, as the most complete cinematic experience. The story of the race presented on the monitor is by contrast audio-visually impoverished, the sound is from the TV monitor, its range of camera set-ups limited, yet, uncannily, it appears at times to match the action seen on the large screen; it seems to be the same race, but isn't. Across these versions, the race slips between documentary and fiction film, displaying the conventions of each as a sound and image *spectacle* of the racing.

Here is a parallel world of racing, with its bets, its proud owners, and its excitement, but which we cannot enter as we might buy a ticket to Ascot. It pleasures with the fiction of cinema through the drama of the races, creating in us the sense of the excitement and exhilaration of the racing, while we enjoy the gravitas of documentary in the vivid and engaging dialogue and accounts of the travellers themselves.

Repeated and varied, and focussed on action – indeed violence as cars crash into each other – the filming of the race makes us aware of the limits of documentary, of both the constructedness of classical documentary and the arbitrariness of what is captured by 'vérité' filming. But we are offered another kind of documentary reality by the three interviews in which the documentary participants – the objects of its gaze and enquiry – speak for themselves as interlocutors with the director who we hear at times, though never see. (She is also heard off-screen in some of the digital video versions of the race.) The different framing of people in medium and long-shot, in fixed spaces of a stables, or a fair, with little editing, seems to mark these scenes as the contingent real, excerpted and incomplete. From these interviews we learn both how the races are set up and what they mean to the travellers who race their horses; but as well we learn something of their place as outsiders transgressing the normal way we expect to use roads, not only in the staging of races but also in their commitment to being travellers, who, as Alan says, have 'never been used to houses', but who are always being told 'Nah, you're not allowed that'. Clio Barnard has commented that 'I see the road race as a form of protest, by winding up the police and taking over the road they are claiming a space for themselves in their identity as travellers – as "King of the Road" for the time of the race – the name given to the "top" horse, the winner of the annual race between the best horses.'

The difference of these episodes of speech and action is paralleled, in a kind of counterpoint, by two gazes foregrounded in the film. One is the 'objective' gaze of the camera at a motorway, busy with speeding vehicles, which appears in two high-angle long-shots from a fixed camera position, each held for some time (around 80 seconds). These are shots of journeying, but they seem like still images because of the fixed camera and the lack of movement on the motorway verges at the edge of the screen frame, which is interrupted centre-frame by a repetitious always-happening but corralled movement of vehicles as a montage within the frame. It is a contemplative gaze of mastery outside of either the fiction or the documentary of the race. These shots frame each version of the race, the opening shot looks towards oncoming traffic, the closing shot shows traffic speeding away, implying the road before and after the event, yet also marking its absence, while the sustained duration of the shot contrasts with the fast editing and close-framing of the race itself.

The other gaze is again two shots, one is at road level showing a corner, intercut with the start of the cinematic race, and the second, a little later, shows the gaze of the woman standing with her dog by the side of the motorway, who turns her head as if watching the race but whom we never see in the same space as the race. This embodied gaze, overlooking, is separated out from the ongoing action of the race, so that it figures here as a stand-in for the camera's look and the future time of our own gaze as embodied spectators. As a woman's gaze, it is in contrast to the wholly male activity of the racing. These inserted shots interrupt the system of repetition and difference both in the race replayed and between its documentary race and its fictional, cinematic race, disturbing the spectacularisation of each and posing on the one hand an objective look, and on the other hand a subjective look, the reverse field of which we are never given. In her interview with Clio Barnard, Emma Cocker suggested that the moment when you realise the cinematically filmed race is a fiction 'is a great revelation, for it seems then that the notion of the embellishment becomes very significant and quite complex. On the one hand it seems to relate to the notion of memory and of memory's embellishment, and on the other it alludes to the myth that surrounds the gypsy traveller culture.' Clio commented, 'I am interested in Jean Rouch's ideas about positioning the filmmaker within the work and taking responsibility in that way. The gypsy word for non-gypsy is gadje, so I am a gadje. I was very aware of that when I was making the piece, and about how difficult it is to represent a culture other than your own. People were angry about the way that they had been misrepresented in the past. There is this duality in that travellers are either presented as a social menace; or the opposite, in relation to a romanticised idea about the nomad… this was very much in my thinking when I was making *Road Race*.'[3]

It is not only documentary film and fictional cinema which are addressed in *Road Race* but also the very way in which we can know the world as we move from the doing and being of what Nietzsche has called the unhistorical of everyday living,[4] in the 'presentational' of the sculptural two-screen and our embodied relation to each, to reflection in a process of remembering. This can become a telling, a representation and organisation of the seen and heard as a relation of causes and effects to become known as knowledge. In *Road Race*, the seen and heard of the being and doing of the racing and of the travellers is never resolved as a point of knowledge, but captures us in the iterations that lure us by their differences and constitute a continuousness, and a continuing of the thought across the stillness and action embodied in each screen. (Images p99)

Elizabeth Cowie

Endnotes:

[1] Carl Andre, writing in reply to a series of questions by Jack Risley and John Zinsser in *Journal of Contemporary Art*. April/May 1990.
[2] Margaret Morse's essay, 'Video Installation Art: The Body, the Image and the Space-in-Between', remains an exemplary exploration of the experience of video installation as 'presentational art', in contrast to the representational. (In Doug Hall and Sally Jo Fifer, eds, *Illuminating Video: An Essential Guide to Video Art* (San Francisco: Aperture in association with the Bay Area Video Coalition, 1991, p153-167.)
[3] Emma Cocker in conversation with Clio Barnard, *Catalogue: Clio Barnard*, Herbert Read Gallery University for the Creative Arts at Canterbury, 2008. My essay here draws on my contribution to the catalogue, edited by Emma Cocker.
[4] Friedrich Nietzsche, *The Use and Abuse of History*, trans. Adrian Collins (New York: The Liberal Arts Press, Bobbs-Merril, 1957), p6.

Pile Up On Levee Road

The paragraph started out like any other, shifted gears, turned a corner too fast, too sharp, ahead of its time, went up over the guard rail and instead of crash, floated down into not exactly collision. There were two disaster tourists gawking at all the christmas crass piled up in the display windows. The story reads like a fifty car pile-up. Paragraphs are made up of words and sentences, as days are made up of minutes and hours. In the aftermath of an accident things very quiet. Just wheels spinning.

The rivalry between France and England can be found in many places. Who has the
most ridiculous signs? Here's a French sign proclaiming:

In order to respect the comfort of our paying customers, the picnic is forbidden on
these premises.

This was at a lonely windswept petrol station under gray skies along the barren stretch of motorway between Belgium and Paris.

Cralan Kelder

mr asbo

500 serfs line the cam
the white bird shouts bakunin
in siren/screech out. bolan
could not write this. feathers tarred
with new labour desk jotting
pen pushing *mr asbo*
type setting club forming out
of M25 sheer
bitterness on an angle
state participation is
beaten on a stagnant wave
anarcho syndicate on
a river bank from bird yet
 to learn he must shut the fuck
up in polite company

Sarah Crewe

The Autoroute and the Picturesque

'The picturesque is found any time the ground is uneven'
(Roland Barthes)¹

On the French Autoroute A75, as you drive through the mountainous Lozèr Auvergne region you meet a road-sign alerting you to the nearby town of Marvejols, a medieval foundation (fig 1: p65). At the foot of its old towered gateway is an enigmatic design based on a modern statue of the legendary Beast of Gevaudan, a monster that in the Eighteenth Century killed hundreds of people in the area, and was even reported to have been active in the 1950s. The sign conjures a world of ancient history, legend and superstition alive in a wild region of the country, and it stands beside that symbol of rational progress, the modern motorway.

This juxtaposition is the kind of thing I am going to discuss: alluring pictures of antiquities and the natural world from the viewpoint of the motorway. How do we relate to what we see of that world and its representations from within the insulated spaces of car and motorway? To what extent has the experience of motorway and its infrastructure – so increasingly a part of our daily lives – been imperceptibly regrinding our cultural lenses over several decades, and reshaping our perception and valuation of landscape and local history?

I'll begin by describing what I think was a watershed in the ways in which, in the western tradition, we have become used to construing landscape. I refer to the vogue for the Picturesque, which came to prominence in England in the late Eighteenth Century. There are two particular points I want to establish about this movement-points that bear on the image you see here in fig 1. Firstly, there is the confrontation between old and new worlds: here it is the presence of the Picturesque medieval towered gateway beside the streamlined modern motorway. Secondly, there is the habit of pictorialising and framing landscape and antiquities, and the special value of them as commodity spectacles. I take the second point first.

The most obvious point to make about the Picturesque is that, as the term implies, it is a means of pictorialising the landscape. In rendering – indeed, in almost *constructing* – landscape as 'scenery' and visual composition, the viewpoint becomes of paramount importance. Eighteenth Century tourists established specific viewpoints, called 'stations'. Stations punctuated tours in the grammar of Picturesque travel. You stopped off at certain points on your carriage, or equestrian or pedestrian tour and paused before a view that satisfied certain aesthetic criteria, borrowed from art criticism and analysis. The criteria related to proportioning of *coulisses*, middle distances, planar recession, graduated light and dark areas, and so on. A view was correctly Picturesque insofar as it conformed with such stipulations, and this in turn was a stimulus to sit and sketch your own version of it.

The precise judgement in fixing the viewpoint was important: not too high, not too low – a little too far to the right or left and the composition would be spoiled. Furthermore it stays a picture as long as you stay still. You don't enter it: you keep it at an appropriate distance, and in so doing you alienate the landscape as spectacle. However, behind this particular formalist aestheticising of landscape, there are certain historical and cultural pressures. This is the other point I want make, and it involves the confrontation between old and modern worlds that the scene of the Marvejols sign offers.

The Picturesque aesthetic in late Eighteenth Century and early Nineteenth Century Britain was in great part a reaction to contemporary developments in urbanisation, agriculture, land enclosures and landscape gardening. In central and southern England vast tracts of uncultivated common land were appropriated and brought under the plough, property boundaries proliferated, invading open land to form the neat patchwork of smoothed fields that became the signature of English landscape. Towns and cities grew their new geometry of terraced housing for the labouring population, crescents and squares for the aristocracy and plutocracy. The intrusive growth of grid developments in town and country by the end of the century stimulated the taste for landscape of a contrary character, one that resisted cultivation and urban settlement, resisted environmental modernisation. Hence the popularity of Picturesque tours to the English Lakes of Cumberland and Westmorland, the Scottish Highlands, mountainous North Wales and the Derbyshire Peak district. In such regions an environment formed by untrammelled organic growth was constructed by Picturesque aesthetics and the attendant tourist industry as a compensatory relief from the formality of new developments elsewhere. An eye increasingly accustomed to a countryside of smooth parkland and thousands of acres of arable land under production, or regularised grid-based city planning became restless for the wild, the accidental, the primitive, the obsolescent. To counter visual boredom, a sensationist concept of visual irritation as a source of pleasure began to creep into theoretical debates on the Picturesque in the 1790s: the idea being that the landscape painter and gardener should provide rugged contours and rough variegated textures for the eye to travel over and be stimulated by. This compensatory aesthetic became very influential. Look at these two bird's eye views: one of a Seventeenth Century country estate in England, Denham Place, Buckinghamshire (circa 1695) (fig 2: p65) and then an 1863 plan of Central Park, New York (fig 3: p66). At Denham Place the estate is designed to be an oasis of order salvaged from Nature's random, unkempt forms in the surrounding hilly landscape. Central Park is designed as almost the opposite. Surrounded by the grid-plan of streets, the Park's designers constituted Nature as relentlessly curvilinear, irregular, and planted with a careful randomness: the park becomes an oasis of relaxed organic forms and unpredictable rhythms, salvaged from the rigid geometry of the city environment.

What we continue to value as 'picturesque' in the vernacular sense – gnarled, old-fashioned, eccentrically angular – have much the same properties. Testimony to the persistence of this aspect of the Picturesque is Roland Barthes's critique of the *Guide Bleu* series, in

Mythologies -: 'The *Blue Guide* hardly knows the existence of scenery except under the guise of the picturesque. The picturesque is found any time the ground is uneven'.² Barthes traces the appeal of unevenness to what he calls the 'old Alpine myth... associated with Helvetico-Protestant morality... a hybrid compound of the cult of nature and of Puritanism (regeneration through clean air, moral ideas at the sight of mountain-tops, summit-climbing as civic virtue, etc)'. This may be partly so, but it leaves out of account the compensatory aesthetic I have been trying to outline – the unease with an over-regulated environment – which was such a very strong component of the English Picturesque. Back in the 1790s, scenery that was rugged and remote – remote culturally and topographically – acquired an aesthetic and then a commercial value: images of wild countryside, as one writer put it, were cherished in proportion as they offered 'an agreeable contrast' to the scenery of the city and domesticated landscape:

> [The landscape painter] was driven into the recesses of the mountains, for subjects of his pencil. From thence he brought home scenes...such as were acceptable to his customers; as forming an agreeable contrast with the ordinary scenery in the environs of cities; the nurseries of arts, and the seats of painting: Indeed, at all times, and everywhere, one great end of Landscape painting is to bring distant scenery, – and such more particularly as is wild and not easily accessible, – under the eye, in a cultivated country... and not to expose itself, by a faint imitation of the views which are seen from the windows of the room, for which the representations are intended as furniture.³

These specific Picturesque qualities were most intensively focussed in ruins – a distillation of those larger aesthetic paradigms. Masonry which was once carefully chiselled and aligned to express a triumph over obstinate material difficulties, now lay broken down by weather, its geometry collapsed, sections of it randomly tufted with grass and flowers. The ruin was an emblem of vengeance on modernity's artifice, a reminder of Nature's formidable 'otherness', and a feast of visual irritation. Ruins had a dual function in traditional iconography: they were melancholy *mementi mori* – reminders that we all face decay and death – but they were mementoes also of nature's supremacy in winning back her territory and materials from construction by line and rule. Their accidental irregularity, like the natural irregularity of uncultivated countryside, became talismanic for the new Picturesque aesthetic of ruggedness.

In the later Eighteenth Century new roads worked their way into those regions most coveted by tourists in search of this kind of Picturesque experience, bringing them smoothly and swiftly into close confrontation with the primitive and the wild, and at the same time these new roads marked the beginning of the end of that primitivism as the influx of new visitors triggered the development of a commercial tourist infrastructure in the heartland of ancient survival cultures.

For a while, around the turn of the century, you could use your summer holiday to step out of the world of Eighteenth Century civilisation into one barely touched by developments since the Middle Ages: the two worlds were closely juxtaposed. These literal tourist passages back and forth between the world of Enlightenment culture and the primitive antique world were enjoyed by those who were already making such transitions imaginatively in their reading. The appetite for an older, rugged culture and environment was stimulated and indulged in the *Tale of Terror* of the 1790s, and a little later, in Walter Scott's historical novels, and the sensationalised confrontation between the modern and primitive worlds was satirically parodied in Jane Austen's *Northanger Abbey*.

I hope what I have been summarising has strong echoes in experiences and mindsets familiar to us today, in the ways we relate to landscape: that is, first, the habit of seeing landscape through real or invisible frames, and through pictures of landscape; and, second, the impulse to construe and value landscape as an aesthetic compensation for an environment increasingly artificial and regularised. Landscape becomes that mythical 'other', an ever-receding alternative environment, voluptuous, autonomous, mysterious. These are powerful, persisting legacies of the Picturesque, still formative in Western aesthetic responses to natural scenery and decaying monuments of past cultures. The Picturesque supplies us with a vocabulary for signifying aesthetic value in our physical environment. We respond strongly to the close juxtaposition of apparently very different worlds (the primitive antique and the modern), and we persist in the habit of pictorialising the landscape, of selecting and signposting particular Picturesque sights. The new highways of late Eighteenth Century England acted as conduits to sites of confrontation between ancient and modern worlds, between nature and culture. The motorway of the late Twentieth Century, together with its infrastructure, has itself become a site of confrontation, as well as the means of travelling to such sites. Let us explore a little further the phenomenon of highway travel.

For the Eighteenth Century traveller, the new roads to remote, primitive regions brought the past quickly within reach of the present – made it accessible. Their descendant, the smooth, sleek highway of today is one of our principal symbols of modernity. It signifies progress, literally and figuratively: it promises freedom, mobility, enlarged commercial and recreational opportunities. It is an emblem of the escape from the old world across whose terrain it streaks so boldly and uncompromisingly. It is an expression of power, just as road-building in the Eighteenth Century had sometimes been. Look for instance at this mid Eighteenth Century painting of Dunham Massey estate, in England, where the landowner expresses the scale and reach of his power in these great radiating avenues across the neighbouring country (fig 4: p66).

The modern motorway has extraordinarily independent powers as it snakes across all kinds of land, burrows through mountains, sails over deep gorges on massive arched viaducts. Motorways are gouged into or stamped onto the land.

Old roads grew slowly out of the landscape, almost organically, from footpaths and carriage tracks, and remained a part of it, conforming to its contours, going round mountains rather than through them, diving steeply into valleys and struggling up out of them, weaving through small villages rather than bypassing them, skirting field boundaries rather than crashing across them. Old roads pulled up frequently for intersections and multiple informal points of access, unlike the limited-access highways with minimal interruptions to rapid progress. Old roads took their time: they deferred to the smaller-scale culture of travel, and to the physical environment they were negotiating. Motorways by comparison are independent of the natural landscape and unresponsive to it.

Once the awesomely brutal engineering operation has completed its trajectory – the dynamiting of cliff-faces, the driving of 1000-foot piles into the valley floors – the road and its users become oblivious of the real contours of the land over which they now skim. They are oblivious in two respects. First, so that vehicles can speed more comfortably to their destinations, motorway construction does its best to neutralise the land's physical unevenness: one hardly relates the surface over which one drives to the surface yards away just off the motorway, and yet it is part of the same terrain. In the light of Barthes' contention that the Picturesque is found any time the ground is uneven, motorways come to epitomise the anti-Picturesque. Secondly they are oblivious because that enhanced speed of passage reduces the time available to register the landscape. It becomes a passing spectacle, and one from which the motorist is relatively insulated.

The French anthropologist, Marc Augé, has described the motorway – like the supermarket and the airport lounge – as one of the 'non-places of supermodernity'. 'If place can be defined as relational, historical and concerned with identity, then a space which cannot be defined as relational, or historical, or concerned with identity will be non-place'.[4] When you are in motorway 'non-place', 'place' itself (dense with history, landscape idiosyncrasy and regional identity –

dense, in effect, with the Picturesque) recedes to an unrolling backdrop. You are aware of it as passing scenery, not traversable surface, even though you are travelling over it and through it. The landscape is virtualised. Augé argues that 'non-place' is where no organic social life is possible. In accommodating ourselves as motorists to this non-organicism, we project organicism onto the landscape flitting by us – that is where it seems to belong. (On long-distance motorway travel we have to come *off* the road in order to meet the needs of our own organic animal constitution: we stop to put food into ourselves, to urinate, or to sleep).

Developments in transport over the last 200 years have had a decisive influence on the way we register and value landscape. Writers, photographers and planners have been exploring this for some time. I want now to explore the ways in which motorway travel bears on, and encourages Picturesque readings of landscape, notably the heightening of that sense of a confrontation between two worlds, and the pictorial packaging of landscape as spectacle. I'm going to be returning, in a while, to those pictorial signs on the French Autoroute for a closer analysis of their function – in particular how they mediate the anticipated experience of the off-motorway world. I choose the Autoroute as the focal study because the signposting there offers the most graphically ambitious and challenging examples that I know of from the road systems in Western Europe and North America, and because that pictorial flamboyance raises particularly interesting issues about Picturesque representation. However, the more general implications that I hope will arise from this particular localised focus should bear on the way we think, in broad terms, about tensions between the natural and the artificial in evaluating our changing environment. First, though, we might consider the experience of viewing landscape – any landscape – from a moving car.

Landscape for the motorist is strongly mediated by frames – the car windows and mirrors – and by the sense one has inside the car of being insulated and independent from the natural world: inflated tires smooth the ride, a powerful engine propels you effortlessly, climate control is adjusted at the turn of a knob. Some interesting studies of the view from the car window have been made by photographers such as Joel Meyerowitz, Lee Friedlander and Patrick Zachmann, and by writers such as Reyner Banham, Peter Osborne and Edward Dimendberg.[5] Reyner Banham's scenic connoisseurship in the Picturesque tradition (but from a moving car) is well illustrated in these remarks about the views in the Mojave Desert, in southern California:

> The scale of the scenery is crucial – if the valley were wider the view would fall apart, if it were more cramped the alternating sequence of broad slopes would lose the stately *adagio* rhythm that gives it such power. I suspect that the whole effect needs also the forward speed of the automobile to bring the alternating slopes into view at the right pace – at walking speed they would be too far apart in time for the congruence of the successive sweeps, the pattern of alternating slopes to be perceived.[6]

Edward Dimendberg, in his essay on cinematic usage of the highway, argues that the 'highway provides a controlled visual experience analogous to the montage and multiplicity of perspectives afforded by cinema'.[7] Landscape from the motorway becomes a movie rather than a collection of stills.

The modern car is a conglomeration of optical modifiers: the mirrors with their convexity slightly distort the scenery they reflect; windscreens and side windows are often slightly tinted to reduce glare. Thus mirrors and windows structurally and chromatically modify the landscape (fig 5: p67).

But stay in the moving car and remove these machine-made frames and lenses and look out on the passing landscape. Roll down the side window and move closer to the sill to look out. What you see – or what you construe – is a polarity: dynamic modern machine-produced geometry in the immediate foreground played off against old nature.

Patrick Zachmann's photograph (one of three) of the Autoroute, 'Motorways, France, 1982' (Magnum, 1982), is a fascinating orchestration of diagonals and horizontals, and a kind of focal chiaroscuro from foreground blur to background definition (fig 6: p67). It appears to be an arbitrary section of motorway view, but is actually carefully composed. It is framed on the left by the horizon tree and blurred support post for the foreground safety barrier, and on the right by the arrival at the vertical of the perspectival hayfield striations.

The dominant lines and angles pull one in contrary directions. The foreground white lines converge, as one scans from right to left, to form a dart pointing in the direction the car is speeding. Above that the perspective lines of the field pull the eye almost in the opposite direction, from left to top right. This sets up a dynamic tension between motorway and outlying countryside – one that is enhanced by other details.

Foreground is all speed and blur. Here is the present of the modern autoroute, difficult to focus. The middle distance has a tense stasis as the great drums of gathered hay are arrested in their apparently rolling movement down the field's slope. The background seems pure stasis. The horizon line is a parallel to the foreground, but 'natural' as against machine-made, and a world away from the hectic movement of the road.

Peter Osborne in commenting on the photograph notes what he calls 'the strata of relative speeds' as one moves from foreground to background.[8] The foreground-to-background recession can be read as a kind of allegory of historical and cultural distancing. There, way beyond 'supermodernity's' concrete, tarmac and metal geometry is the primal natural stillness of trees, fields and sky. The latter idyll is an illusion, of course, because the field's form will change as the annual cycle continues: that tree is growing and will die. But the flash-by gaze of the motorist doesn't imaginatively register processes: spectacle, and desultory rapid sequence, is all – a kind of extended 'visual irritation'. And it is as spectacle that landscape is dramatically constituted.

This is just what the Autoroute signs connive at, in their more diagrammatic, explicit way. They underpin the effect of motorway travel as an experience of alienating landscape, both visually and culturally. They are a constant reminder of what we might be missing by choosing to travel in this way – by choosing to spend more of our lives in 'non-place'.

The Autoroute signs offer large, rectangular framed pictures of desirable sights – not too detailed – just detailed enough for safe absorption at 130 kilometers per hour. They anthologise, pictorially process and situate the experience of landscape for the motorist in such a way as to suggest worlds culturally distant from the immediate present of the Autoroute. They reinforce that sense of dualism which is so characteristic of the Picturesque program, antiquity and modernity, haphazard ruggedness and smooth engineered precision. These are framed glimpses of the Other.

Look at what they offer. Saint-Flour (fig 7: p68) is an ancient hilltop town, an organic social and architectural growth over several centuries, Picturesquely rugged and unevenly textured in its pyramidal profile, thrusting out of its signboard frame. This is an antithesis of the Autoroute.

These signs, in reminding the motorist of an older world now being bypassed, reinforce that broader experience of landscape from the moving car, as imaged in Zachman's photograph.

The pictorial signs belong to a different category of signposting from the purely directional or otherwise functional information on the Autoroute – the alerts to imminent rest-areas, or *Aires*, and their iconised facilities, or the boards advertising the varying prices for fuel at the next service stations. Such signposting is on a blue or white background. The pictorial signs are uniformly brown. The colour distinction is a significant marker of functional difference. Brown signs don't challenge you to make navigational decisions: you don't have to *do* anything with them.

They alert the traveller to distinctive landscape features, historical sites or towns and villages (which may or may not be visible from the Autoroute), and they do it by translating topographical identity into attractive imagery. Blue and white signs will help you get to these off-Autoroute places, the brown signs show you what you might see once you get there, or how you might imagine it: they evoke rather than designate. A case in point is the sign for the 'bataille de Crecy', (fig 8: p68) showing a scene from the 1346 battle.

A medieval archer on a hillside takes aim across the Autoroute. Banners, helmets, armour – a forlorn glimpse of medieval pageantry abuts on the tarmac and concrete highway, and briefly draws the eye across the flat fields around it. Was this visible landscape, precisely, the spot where the French and English engaged centuries ago? Or was it nearby but out of sight? The romantic suggestiveness of medieval battle, swords, shields and knights in armour, is in such contrast to this demure, dull agricultural landscape.

Marc Augé has identified the French Autoroute system as almost diagrammatic of the relationship between 'non-place' and place. French towns and villages have historically asserted their organic structures, their town centres are concentrations of traditional, rooted social and civic life – church and church square, market square, Mairie, monuments to townsfolk lost in two World Wars. The network of highways links these centres across France, and increasingly roadsigns textually and pictorially elaborate the specific identity of the town:

> [They advertise] fourteenth or fifteenth-Century chapels, castles and palaces, megaliths, museums of crafts, lace or pottery. Historical depth is vaunted… Every town or village

Fig 1: Marvejols p53

Fig 2: Denham Place, Buckinghamshire (circa 1695) p55

Fig 3: 1863 plan of Central Park, New York p55

Fig 4: mid-Eighteenth-Century painting of Dunham Massey estate p58

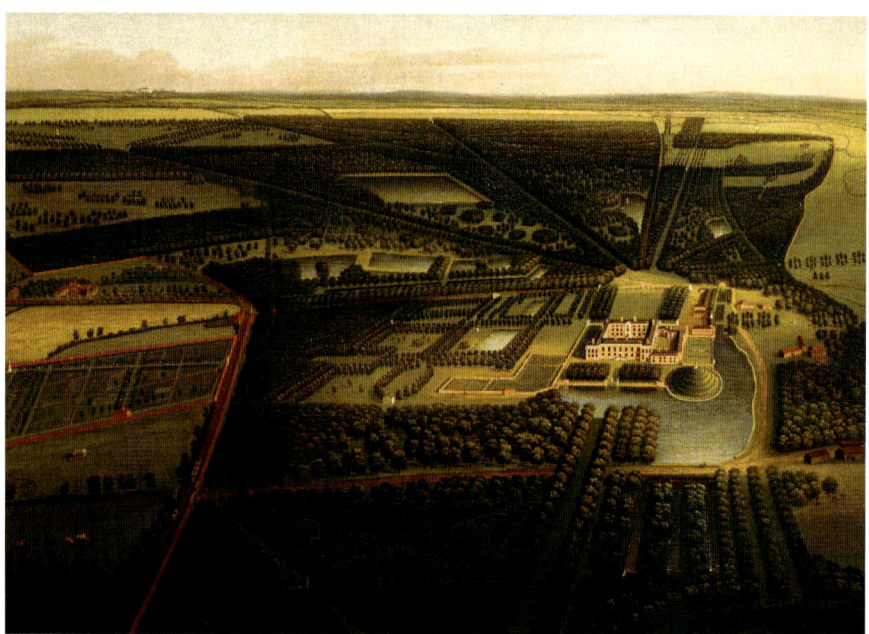

Fig 5: 'windows structurally and chromatically modify the landscape' p61

Fig 6: Patrick Zachmann's photograph (one of three) of the Autoroute, 'Motorways, France, 1982' (Magnum, 1982) p62

Fig 7: Saint-Flour p63

Fig 8: Sign for the 'bataille de Crecy', showing scene from the 1346 battle p64

Fig 9: Villages de l'Aubrac p73

Fig 10: p74

Fig 11: p74

Fig 12: The sign highlights the famous white Charolais cattle p75

Fig 13: Severac-le-Chateau p76

Darenth Interchange, A2/M25 Junction; Kent. 2011. Photo by Edward Chell

Gesso Panels by Edward Chell. Acrylic and Lacquer on Gesso.
Each panel 28 cm x 23 cm (11" x 9") Date 2011

Conium maculatum

Broken Umbellifer

Dipascus fullonum

Senecio jacobaea

not of recent origin lays public claim to its history, displaying it to the passing motorist on a series of signboards which add up to a sort of 'business card'. Making the historical context explicit in this way...coincides with a reorganization of space (the creation of bypasses and main motorway routs avoiding towns) that tends, inversely, to short-circuit the historical monuments that embody it.[9]

For Augé, the 'non-places' of supermodernity are partly defined by their being empty of history. Early Twentieth Century modernity, in his argument, could still interweave the old and the new, but supermodernity is a more radical rupture from the old organic world, and it 'makes the old (history) into a specific spectacle, as it does with all exoticism and all local particularity'.[10] The Autoroute pictorial signposting is both a symptom and an agent of this process. How do the signposts relate motorway to landscape, the present to the past? They tend to radicalise the separation in a number of ways.

The signposts can be *performative*, not just referential and descriptive; and sometimes explicitly performative, as when ramblers are depicted setting off into the countryside, and bidding the motorist to do the same. Look at the left alignment of the hiker in the 'Villages de l'Aubrac' sign (fig 9: p69) and remember the Picturesque rules about 'stations', the relation of the tourist-viewer to the pictured scene, and the need to keep outside the frame in order to preserve the picture. Something sensational is happening on the 'Villages de l'Aubrac' sign: the hiker-tourist is out of the frame and *walking into a picture*. She is in 'non-place', like us, and is walking into 'place'.

If you were to follow this hiker's example and head for Picturesque Aubrac, the region's website ('Bienvenue sur le portail de l'Aubrac') would draw you knee-deep into fields of daffodils, immersed in a synthetic rural idyll, a composite of old stone buildings, figures working the soil: everything speaks of a timeless, slow, quiet, pre-industrial idyll, a world away from the concrete and tarmac highway, and the roar of traffic. Aubrac constitutes its attractiveness in

Picturesque terms by promoting everything that is antithetical to the Autoroute.

So these signs can be performative. They can also be *constitutive*. The Autoroute experience of France's distinctiveness, on the route from Calais to the Mediterranean, via Paris, Orleans and Clermont-Ferrand, shrinks to an anthology of places of historical, scenic or commercial interest. It reconfigures France. In his essay 'The *Blue Guide*', Roland Barthes argued that the Blue Guide to Spain reduces the country to an oversimplified typology: 'the Basque is an adventurous sailor, the Levantine a light-hearted gardener, the Catalan a clever tradesman... The ethnic reality of Spain is thus reduced to a vast classical ballet'. The land itself is crudely essentialised as a web of mainly religious monuments:

> To select only monuments suppresses at one stroke the reality of the land, and that of its people, it accounts for nothing of the present, that is, nothing historical, and as a consequence, the monuments themselves become undecipherable, therefore senseless.[11]

The Autoroute signs inscribe the *Blue Guide* effect onto the motorway landscape and map its typology. For instance, the broad Aubrac region is iconised into a cow and an old dry-stone barn in treeless high country.

Barthes' complaint was that the *Blue Guide* reduced Spain to a display case of old religious monuments and thereby suppressed both its historical dynamic and its contemporary vitality and diversity. The Autoroute signs, while enacting similar patterns, are less uniform. They may emphasise French history and traditional rural ways of life, but they also represent contemporary commercial identity. Thus for instance as the Autoroute approaches Montlucon, signs represent its scenic and historical attractions as well as its industrial identity – separate pictorial displays for each, signifying the coexistence of a thriving economy with a respect for the environmental and architectural legacy (figs 10: p69 and 11: p70).

That traditionally tense relationship between commerce and old-world idyll is brought into closer juxtaposition when the traveller is welcomed into Bourbon country not far from Montlucon. This is distinctive 'bocage', a countryside of small fields and hedges which concentrates on the rearing of cattle for the dairy and meat markets. The sign highlights the famous white Charolais cattle (fig 12: p70). On the right panel is a timeless pastoral scene, with cattle grazing and drinking. On the left the cow has become a meat menu, a subject for discriminating butchery. One side is happy pastoral, the other is commerce. One side aesthetic and the other side utilitarian. But of course these antitheses are culturally constructed. Both panels promote commodities of a kind, in two senses. First of all, the rearing of cattle in the idyllic *bocage* is a farming industry, costly on resources of time and money; neither cattle nor fields really belong to Nature. Secondly, the pastoral-aesthetic idyll in the right panel has become appropriated as yet another commercial amenity in the tourist economy – the Picturesque.

* * *

The speed, smoothness and facility of Autoroute journeys through the landscape enhance the sense of our being increasingly distanced from the past and strengthen that sense of a 'lost myth' that Picturesque tourists for over two centuries have associated with landscape and antiquity. Progress, of which the Autoroute is one of the great symbols, is by definition a pulling away from the past: in the process we are alienated from the direct experience of natural landscape, of living and working with it and in it, of travelling over its uneven surface. We have looked at some of the ways in which the Autoroute experience mediates and indeed reconstitutes landscape as a visitable spectacle. The framed pictorial signs are continuous with the experience of viewing through the car window frames: they promote environmental features and activities that increasingly acquire a novelty value for those increasingly inured to life lived in the 'non-place' of Autoroute. The Autoroute has become the great bypass of history and idiosyncratic place, both of which become iconised in the language of the Picturesque.

The French are rather more flamboyant in drawing attention to the remote Picturesque attractions of their country. The mysterious otherness of 'La France Profonde' has a kind of mythical meaning for the national identity. It is otherwise in England, where motorway signposting is concerned. Indeed brown signs on their own (as opposed to small brown panels within the larger, blue directional signs) are hardly present on the motorways. British tourist signing policy is altogether more constrained than in France, by factors such as minimal visual distraction for the motorist who might be travelling at 60 or 70miles per hour, a tariff of the minimum visitor numbers necessary for a site to qualify for motorway signposting, and a highly stylised and uniform design formula for the signs themselves. It is recognised, with a nice irony, that tourist signs themselves can have 'a cumulative detrimental impact on the environment', and especially on those areas of scenic beauty which they might be trying to highlight to the traveller.[12]

* * *

When we stop on the Autoroute and get out of our cars for refreshment, the same perceptual habits persist, the same modes of representation and consumption of landscape.

I will close with one example: Severac-le-Chateau (fig 13: p71). This is a relatively new *Aire* in the Aveyron (17 hectares, opened in June 1998), and is situated so as to take full Picturesque advantage of a beautiful landscape feature, the Eleventh Century castle of Severac on an adjacent hill. Four million people stop there every year.[13] It is a powerful means of projecting old-world, regional France. The café is sited to take in the huge panorama of that countryside. Just as if one were inside the car, one can sit with one's cappuccino, in air-conditioned comfort, and admire a sumptuous framed view of the old world. Without being artificially reproduced, nature and antiquity have been appropriated to café décor, just as their representations have been appropriated for Autoroute décor. We should recall those remarks made by the Picturesque critic William Marshall 200 years ago, when he commented prescriptively on late Eighteenth Century attitudes to landscape, and its appropriation, domestication and spectacle-making:

> at all times, and everywhere, one great end of Landscape painting is to bring distant scenery, – and such more particularly as is wild and not easily accessible, – under the eye, in a cultivated country... and not to expose itself, by a faint imitation of the views which are seen from the windows of the room, for which the representations are intended as furniture.[3]

Wild countryside and cultivated rooms. If we juxtapose the café room's window-framed view of the ancient hill town with the earlier road-sign picture of St-Flour, the Autoroute's Picturesque mediation of landscape and history becomes very clear. The eye in a cultivated country, and the representations of wild scenery compensatorily adorned rooms deprived of access to such landscapes.

Rooms can take many forms. The camera is, etymologically, a room – a 'chamber', with a lens on the outside world. A car is a mobile room. By extension, the Autoroute becomes a kind of room, a corridor. The Autoroute's framed pictures, liminally perched between motorway and landscape, adorn the invisible walls of our long, monotonous, 'non-place' corridors.

Malcolm Andrews

Endnotes:

[1] Roland Barthes, 'The *Blue Guide*': *Mythologies* Tr Annette Lavers, Paladin, 1973, p74.
[2] Roland Barthes, *op cit.*, p74.
[3] William Marshall, *A Review of The Landscape, A Didactic Poem: also of An Essay on the Picturesque: together with Practical Remarks on Rural Ornament* 1795.
[4] Marc Augé, *Non-Places: Introduction to an Anthropology of Supermodernity*, tr John Howe, Verso, London & New York, 1995, pp77-8.
[5] See Peter D. Osborne, *Travelling Light: Photography, Travel and Visual Culture*, Manchester University Press, 2000, esp. Ch 9.
[6] Reyner Banham, *Scenes in America Deserta*, Thames & Hudson, 1982, p.149
[7] Edward Dimendberg, 'The Will to Motorisation: Cinema, Highways, and Modernity', *October* 73 (Summer 1995), p107.
[8] Peter D.Osborne, *op cit*, p171
[9] Marc Augé, *op cit*, p68
[10] *Ibid*, p110
[11] Roland Barthes, *op cit*, pp75,76.
[12] *Traffic Signs to Tourist Attractions and Facilities in England: Tourist Signing - Trunk Roads.* Design Manual for Roads and Bridges, Volume 8, Section 2, Part 4: TD 52/04. The Stationery Office, 2004.
[13] Information from Website: http://www.severac-le-chateau.com/angl1.html

The Road to Romance

Bedroom door closes before Milton Keynes
Atomised passion tamps under artic axles
Our heroine pants at Keele or Knutsford
Fingers his last letter, coffee untouched
Tears beyond green gas holder at Bescot
Bronzed hunks are striding
Not to Walsall or Wolverhampton
A million bosoms heave, the press of tyre treads
You drive straight through broken hearts
Get over it, girl
Put your foot down.

John Calvert

When A to B is not the point...
The Nocturnal Geography
of the Motorway Service Station

Introduction

This project is a cartography of the <u>un</u>-visible, a geography of the quotidian, and a documentation of cars, people, transactions and space. It is concerned with transient human migration across micro spaces, and particularly with social activities which take place in the night-time hours at motorway service stations — those roadside conurbations of cafés, toilets, shops and parking areas located at intervals along superhighways for the convenience and safety of travellers.

These spaces invite observation and documentation in order to better understand how their hidden lives extend beyond the everyday and add to narratives of people and place, cultural and individual memory. The phenomenon of these places and the activities which they shelter contribute brief but meaningful stories to the odyssey of modern travel, and become our own fragments of road folklore.

Of all the practices which feature in the night-time geography of the service station, I am considering one group here: social and commercial human transactions. These include amorous encounters, drug-dealing, trafficking and music culture.

Why? Firstly because for me there is a particular poignancy when issues of gender, love and sex, boundary shifts and crossings, commerce and covert exchanges are played out in these restless zones of banality and consumption. Secondly, I want to explore how these choreographies and scenes of everyday relationships might be recorded as geography.

We are looking into an intimate underworld; here are momentary actions, pick-ups and drop-offs. They are no easier to catch and label than the pied wagtails dancing over the service station car parks at dusk. So, for the present, the shorthand I am using to construct this story features film images and 'pulp' novels. My aim in doing this is to focus our attention, because these collected images and words are rich with the ingredients of the story, and they are no less fantastical than the reality of the service station. Supporting research has included mapping, field work, participant observation, evidence-based practiceand a lot of late night dining.[1]

In the vehicle, the driver is at one with the machine, in a travelling bubble subject to fine control. But when the individual leaves the temperature regulated, self selected soundtrack, seat adjusted, centrally locked cocoon of the car at the motorway service station, disorder beckons; danger and intimacy collide. Whilst it seems gargantuan and in plain sight, its situation off the main line, foot-down and keep moving strip of the motorway, gives the service station a particular isolation. Here, the fleeting contact of city life mixes with the intimacy of the local.[2] It is the most peripheral outpost of the metropolitan drifter, and a nexus for the suburban seeker after company, with nowhere else to go.

At night, these nameless places with their pointless machines continue a perfunctory existence, but the orbits of cars and people and commerce are joined by other activities, of desire, of remembering and forgetting, in a febrile film which distorts and blurs the ordinary image of the roadside rest stop. It is a place where novelty and obsolescence enjoy an uneasy coupling, where the transience is permanent, and where the evidently controlled environment of commerce and closed circuit television is punctured by other impulses and transactions which, in this memory-less context, hang in the air for but moments after actant and actor meet and part.[3] Then, the motorway service station is a place of phantoms and fantasies, imaginings and vanishings where, quoting John Berger 'in the evening, Pleasure and Desolation take their evening stroll... and walk hand in hand'.[4] It is both glamorous *and* distressed, a magnet for illicit meetings and an opportunity for stepping out of normal life.

Day

An achievement of the Romans in Britain, were their *Mansio* waystations spaced a day's march apart and providing all the facilities desired and needed by travellers: food, lodging, vehicle repairs, and entertainment including on-site brothels.[5] They were succeeded by coaching inns – roadside hostelries equipped to service the needs of humans and horses. As coaching inns entered the itineraries of motor car travellers in the early Twentieth Century, stables gave way to garages, spit and sawdust bars to tea rooms.

Britain came late to building high speed roads. A key point of persuasion to release the massive expenditure for new roads was their comparative safety. To promote safety, regular stopping places were necessary for both human and vehicular relief and refreshment. There were no speed limits from 1959, when the first part of M1 opened, until 1965, making the motorway a new and exciting space for anyone with personal transport. The private commercial businesses which developed and operated the service stations saw the opportunities presented by captive audiences coming in off the highway.[6] What the operators built to house their services drew on the more flamboyant tectonic and decorative expression of Italian and north American installations.

Instantly the motorway service station was the place to be, and be seen. Bringing tungsten day into backwoods Britain, it offered all night service, and a place to play. Cafeterias and steak grills provided clipped neat hostesses to meet the drivers; chefs and waitresses brought hotel style dining to hungry travellers. From these glamorous venues, brightly coloured postcards were dispatched to loved ones, announcing the sender's participation in this super-modern context. Looking into these luminous views to discover their stories, we see groomed bodies and unblemished surfaces drifting in a blankly superficial modern space, somewhere on a spectrum between business and leisure, anticipation and bemusement paralleling the emptiness of an Edward Hopper[7] painting. What we don't see is the underworld of bodies and shadows, shifted out from the cities to these new borderlands, seeding the stories which haunt the service station.

Fifty years on, motorway day is hard cold chromed and synthetic, a chemical thin crust of commerce. As concentrations of urban activity placed in rural contexts, service areas bring with them what George Simmel has called the tempo and multiplicity of economic, occupational and social life. Travellers become vectors multiplied by velocity and compressed by time. Iain Sinclair found his drift into the edge-land of the services 'clean, tactfully lit, unendurable. Everything is designed to get you out of there within minutes of finding a table... It's not day or night. You're completely disoriented'.[8] A visit to the motorway services forms a routine circuit of consumption tracing capitalism itself, in its constant remaking of the present, its preoccupation with the immediate future and the expectation of forthcoming gratification.[9] In his poem 'Gymnasium', Simon Armitage presents the loneliness of the treadmill runner, going nowhere fast. He sees the sun-less squash courts, boredom, loneliness, and the solitude and pathos of pointless repetition in the exercise room.[10] The relationship between body, machine and action, and Armitage's metaphors of ennui, are paralleled in the service station: the endless cycles of drive in-drive out, buy-drink-pee-flush, defrost-fry-serve on autopilot. Alongside this brisk turnaround of trade, are gambling, sugar and caffeine giving impetus to the boredom and stimulating free running reveries as a reaction to motorway solipsism. Here are the last-chance selling activities of the fairground, dazzling and tawdry. But beyond the gaze, what?

To see untarnished motorway glamour, the bright dawn which formed our present motorway night, we need to visit the Autostrada del Sole near Bologna, Italy, circa 1964. In *Cantagallo*, the only feature film focussed entirely on life at the motorway services (and made by British Petroleum to sell itself to users of the Italian Autostrada), travellers and locals converge.[11] Establishing shots show the restaurants bridging the multi-lane highway, thronged with staff, busy with shoppers and diners. The storyline of a parted and reunited couple tracks the twenty four hour operation of the service station and carries us from day into night, when formality softens and conversations begin. Incidentally, couples often feature in filmic trips to the services, as though finding an anonymous tableau in which to concentrate their relations. In the early hours of the morning, this couple argue and separate, each journeying away we know not where: him by car, she by coach. Lost in remorse, lost on the highway, the trajectories of the two converge serendipitously at the Cantagallo *MottaGrill* site. Our couple find themselves hidden from each other by speeding traffic, but then she misses her bus. He gazes into, and beyond the vehicle stream. There she is flesh beyond the tarmac: 'Maria? Maria! Maria!'. 'Franco, Franco'.

The bridge of the service building is a metaphor for reunion, and celebration. As we return to the circular routines of the motorway, Maria and Franco disappear from view. Day transits into night. Quick-stop visitors are detained by dinner, and our couple remerge still celebrating their luck. How curious motorway time is, given that it was their afternoon a few film frames previously. A celebratory champagne supper is shared with young lovers across the room – two slow-motion islands of amour amidst the tide of travellers. We end this film, and make our own move into darkness with a night scene of the service station, now very evidently a place with its own stories and memories.

Night

Motorway night is shapeless and endless. Motorway night is velvet soft enough to put your hand into, rich with the possibility of stepping into it, evaporating. And motorway night seeps into the service station building with every arriving and departing visitor, blurring and smearing time and awareness. This is what the night brings, the tightly controlled confines of the service area giving way to a permissive dislocation from reality; another world happening beneath the sheen. The individualised actions of pleasure seekers (which are concomitant with the complexities of metropolitan culture) create a topography of sensation. Other transactions are performed, the ritual inverse of daylight anonymity.

The motorway service area evolved out of the transport café, and indeed until the late 1990s many still provided a café exclusively for truckers. So the service area took the all-night café culture of the city to rural locations on a significant scale. It inherited the role of night-time meeting place, informal members' club and playground: youths easing into the dark, motor cyclists out for a run, lovers and seekers after love, sex workers, and others involved in covert or illegal activities.

In *Hell Drivers*[12] and *The Leather Boys*,[13] all night cafes are resorts for groups identifying themselves as outlaws. *Hell Drivers* assembles a team of wild truck drivers battling on the roads with each other and innocent motorists, accounting for each day's exploits in a wayside pull-up. *The Leather Boys* introduces us to a north-west London motor cycling community centred on the Ace Café in Stonebridge Park. We experience the geography of the quasi-domestic catering interior contrasting with the indeterminate darkness of the vehicle park, intense camaraderie of a common passion and the road. Both films use the placelessness of the road to challenge foregoing filmic stereotypes of masculinity too, and centre on the nuances of key relationships, in a setting of youth, speed and violence. My broken backed copy of *Chopper: England's King of the Angels*, reprises the primary couplings which drive these stories: two men in physical, gladiatorial opposition.[14] They compete through speed and performance, they brawl and embrace, with death as the consummation. Motor cycle groups and chapters would congregate at the motorway services, arriving in echelons to share stories, play the jukebox, and occasionally fighting or stealing furniture. With these tragic-heroic, nihilistic insights, we add to the understanding of how social territories at the roadside are defined, and can be mapped. As youths formed music groups in the late 1950s, the motorway became an obvious place to meet and exchange news and knowledge. Fans soon discovered this was the place to find their pop stars too. With mass leisure markets so sex followed...[15] Groupies would hitch to the services to hang out, be driven off in a van by one group, and then dropped off to another group. The cavalcade engaged service station workers too, waitresses remembering how staff slept with customers, 'even the manager was at it'.

If films *Hell Drivers* and *The Leather Boys* speak of the human congregation in spaces at the roadside, then *Charlie Bubbles* introduces a different dynamic.¹⁶ Albert Finney's directorial debut is contemporary with *Cantagallo*, but is instead poised at the junction between utopian modernism and dystopian reality, reflecting the mood of the Britain in which it was made. As the eponymous lead character, Finney is tired by having everything, and his ennui clouds this journey between glamour, nostalgia and the remoteness of contemporary life. Bubbles heads north from London one night with his secretary/girlfriend (an early film role for Liza Minelli), and pauses at Newport Pagnell motorway service station on M1.

Here, amidst the plastic lined transatlantic glamour of the Fortes' cafeteria in the small hours of the morning, Bubbles meets the family he has left behind for his career. Dressed formally yet with no apparent destination, the seated group of ex-wife, child, associates and strangers is in markedly isolated territory. They remind us of an earlier scene in the film where Bubbles contemplates a series of closed circuit television screens monitoring each part of his house. In life and in public, the individuals are no less objectified or separate in their propinquity. At the motorway services they are adrift too from the references of daytime and other travellers and from society too.

Ron Peck contemplates the painting 'Nighthawks' of 1942 in his short film *Edward Hopper*, and comments that for himself the late night diner – the subject of Hopper's painting – is 'somewhere to go in all that blackness – a bolthole'.¹⁷ Peck took 'Nighthawks' as the title for his 1978 film depicting, for the first time in Britain, the everyday life of a metropolitan gay man. *Nighthawks* mingles the precarious intimacy of the gay disco with the anonymous security of the motorway service area, because it is in the latter place that the lead character chooses to 'come out' to his female colleague: they are in private amongst a crowd of strangers. With *Nighthawks* the service station becomes a three-dimensional metaphorical backdrop for an underground life. As the character says: 'I enjoy going out, on my own, without any ties, not knowing whom I'm going to meet, where I'm going to end up...'[18]

The pursuit of places which are other than everyday, and which can be appropriated for transient use, is a feature of activity in the arena of male same sex desire. Service station washrooms, like the café toilets and shower rooms before them, are useful meeting places – accessible and anonymous – supplanting the railway stations of Oscar Wilde's time. To understand how the service station forms a locus for the meeting of men by men for sex, we can look to the truck stops of North America which have featured in much textual material from pulp novels and magazines.

Geographies are perhaps understood as something tangible, physically *there* in place, but the meeting of men with men is predicated on the construction of alternative identities, fantastical 'scenes' and assemblages of personal and physical characteristics, all with their own visual codes. As important venues of modernity, the link between service station toilets and cruising is well established because they provide an anonymous meeting territory where fantasies can be played out. There are many examples in gay erotic fiction which give a textual impression of these particular spatial uses. *Hot Tricks* is an anthology of male encounters in the context of machine – trucks, motorcycles, jukeboxes and pinball tables.[19] It creates a particular frisson in which the direct expression of impulsive needs and unmet longings is given prominence. Its drifting locations and multiplicity of gasoline and spittle connections between cowboy truckers, hobos and hitch-hikers are deliberately cast as forgone legends, mysteries protecting the self, but urging the genre into a romanticised history of places and bodies made real by their meetings.

Besides recreational sexual activities, service stations are sites for commercial sexual transactional activities – people becoming the ultimate impulse purchase. Selling sex for gain, part of the roadside

M56: poem by Angela Keaton

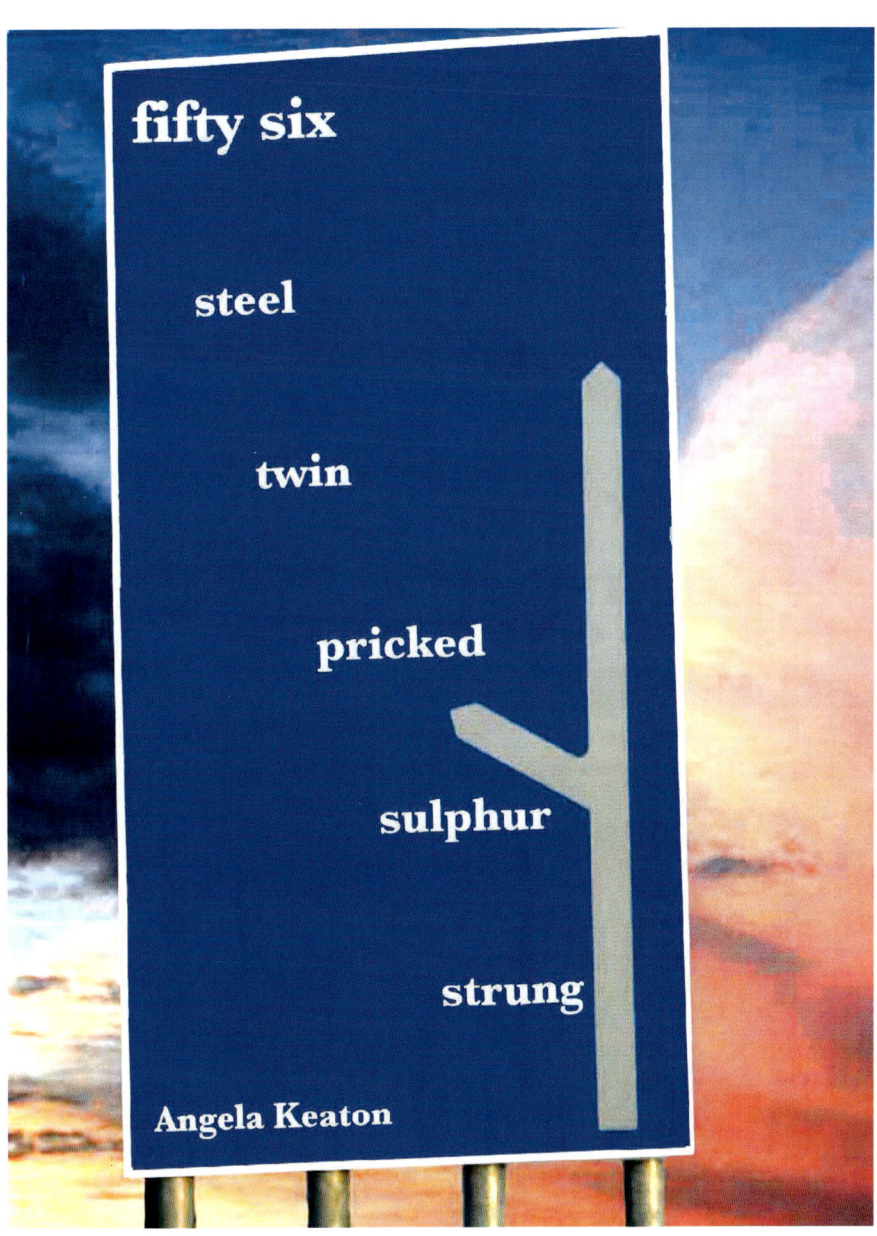

Bird's eye view of a motorway junction: Mike Webb (p15)

Hilton Park at night: David Lawrence

'Road Race', Clio Barnard, 2005; Elizabeth Cowie (p41)
– The Driver:

– Road Race Dave

Footbridge: Forton at night: David Lawrence

industry since the Romans, is a complex transaction, involving thoughts, feelings, emotions, fantasy, desire and loneliness. (Characteristics of eroticism and solitude have long been co-opted by the advertising industry to sell cars, and which have been themes in road stories and movies.) The night-time motorway service station provides the perfect void into which to project such phenomena. With the closure of houses for working girls under legislation aimed at tackling organised crime, so the girls have moved onto the streets, and out to the service station. It is safer than street walking. The better sites extend a benign tolerance to sex workers. Websites and message boards continue to draw men to motorway sites.[20] These online presences offer their own mapping systems, notes and criteria linked to Google maps or other systems, offering co-ordinates to make the cruising grounds points of interest on in-car GPS receivers. A number of websites offer the potential for posting meetings. Those aimed at men seeking women frequently use avatars constructed from random personal data and images, digital sirens calling travellers to obsolete virtual landscapes.[21] In the physical world, service areas on international trucking routes are lucrative for prostitution.[22]

The landscape of the service station, with its centralisation of human services surrounded by vehicle parking, slip roads and fragments of abandoned or unused ground, make them ideal for informal sexual practices including cottaging and dogging.[23] More cottaging has moved to the services since public conveniences in towns have closed. There is a whole community of people committed to it, and integrating it with their lives. They make road trips and odysseys regularly, hunting pleasure and fleeing recognition. How far need one drive? Is there a precise journey point where there is maximum anonymity and expediency? In the service station toilets the necessary gear is here too: prophylactics, disposable tooth brushes (now with caffeine/energy boosters), aftershave and breath fresheners. With the advent of online dating, men who wanted to meet other men were anchored to their homes but better able to sift through potential hook-ups.[24] The advent of the smart phone and specialized GPS location-based apps has changed the waiting to a search governed by the pulse of the texting thumb, and the imperative of the instant message.[25] Not all service station meetings are for sex. Transgender individuals find the anonymous yet public setting a haven for social gatherings. Men become women for the evening, perhaps only twenty miles from home but a lifetime away from their everyday personas.[26]

Returning to the theme of human isolation implicating the motorway services, we find it amplified in other films. *Radio On*, the first English road movie, sees a late-night loner glide out of London on the elevated motorway to a west London service station.[27] The character's brief night-time getaway from a troubled relationship, involves only him and an array of machines: a westward arc of human, vehicular and electronic movements complemented by the synthetic music of Kraftwerk and David Bowie. Captured by camera and played out across screens (movie screen, windscreen and cathode ray), *Radio On* offers a pre-digital layering of spatial data mapping a physical and emotional nowhere close to all of us. It also defines something of the nature of the English road movie in contrast to the American version: here the country is small, and even when there is nowhere to go you soon run out of road. There, the night is a clamour of neon entreaties to dine and sleep; here, it is an assignation with spectres and short-lived dreams.

Music and motorways recur, in actuality and in movies. If *Radio On* was poised on the shift of Britain into full-tilt conservatism, then the next role of the services was poised absolutely in the midst of the hedonistic Thatcher years. Mobile phones began as car phones, which in the late 1980s were cumbersome gadgets useless outside the car. Organisers of warehouse parties utilised the anonymous banks of public telephones in service stations to communicate locations of their secret gatherings. As messages were relayed, so cars raced from one roadside restaurant to the next, in staged advances to the venue. Membury and Heston services (both M4), Knutsford and Hilton Park (both M6), make good gathering places before and after the parties, until the accretion of cars blocking traffic alerts the police. For the dancers – 'ravers' – day and night merged under electrical and physical constellations.

In the 1990s recession a generation of bored teenagers sought out the motorway vehicle parks to perform vehicle stunts for each other, their activities clouded by the ectoplasm of smoking rubber made blood red by assembled tail lights.

Popular crime stories include the service station. Service areas on the new motorway south west of Manchester form pivotal points in the storyline of *Girl on the M6*.[28] When an off duty policeman travels home in his new luxury Jaguar car, he is overtaken by 'a fire engine red Mini... a fleeting glimpse of her sitting forward over the wheel, a fair-haired girl'. Stopping at Knutsford for an early lunch, the officer shares a table and cigarette with the blonde. She leaves, he discovers a notebook she has dropped and becomes observer to a sequence of burglaries and murders which share the armature of the motorway and visits to the service stations for exchange of contraband. Tracking the chronology of highway trips, the policeman charts the criminal gang's location. Justice and death come to the felons in a suburb at the edges of the highway – the isolated dwelling mirroring the bleak modernity of the cafeteria where his sleuthing began – and the blonde is saved.

Not all are redeemed by a visit to the service station. 'Yorkshire Ripper' Peter Sutcliffe regularly returned to a restaurant built on an escarpment cut through by motorway M1. From this benign alpine cabin he could access the eastern slopes of the Pennines and journey out to make his killings, and here he discarded a home-made weapon which was to be evidence in his trial. *The Vanishing* brings relationships, loss and death into the geography.[29] Bound for a romantic motor tour of southern France, a Dutch couple pause briefly for refreshment and to share the driving. What could go wrong for lovers Rex and Saskia, at a motorway service area where each element – discrete, enclosed and visibly legible – is in its place?

With a flirty run across the car park, the girl goes for cold drinks and is detained by a man seemingly in need of help with his car. Keen to speak some French, full of love and adventure, the girl agrees. Seated in his car, reality returns as she is overcome and loses consciousness to his concealed chloroform. The vanishing has taken time, but there is no trace of the girl. It becomes a question of how the boyfriend surveys the scene, concealed by crowds and moving vehicles, how his viewpoint and the objective truth are masked by the manifest banality of the site. We know that his girlfriend's drugging and abduction was possible precisely because of the flow of transient people, and the apparent ordinariness. For the remaining lover, only by reviewing the place through a Polaroid and triangulating the facts by speaking to others, does another story emerge: 'Once more he looked at the photograph... Once more. Systematically he sifted the building for her possible presence... She seemed to have vanished from the face of the earth'.[30] Again, as day rolls into night, the despair multiplies. 'To want to sleep, to be unable to sleep, to sleep, it all merged into a single thought: Something dreadful was happening to Saskia at this very moment.'[31]

Summoned by the murderer with the promise of a truth to be revealed, Rex returns to the service station, the night and the rain. We are held captive there too, at the edge of the car park and far from the lights of the café. The revelation of the mystery begins and ends in a muddle of water and earth and sodium lights, as darkness envelops all. *The Vanishing* proposes a horror fantasy, but it's worth noting that in reality, contemporary night-time thefts from commercial vehicles, may be accomplished by rendering the sleeping driver unconscious by gassing.[32]

We end our journey with another example of lovers separated by the poetry and horror of the motorway night.

In *Honeymoon*, a bride is abandoned by her husband just after their wedding.[33] She spends a night alone in a service station at Christmastide, the only consummation being immersion in a reverie which is by turn magical and terrifying, as the bride stumbles upon the lost, drifters, transgender individuals, and aggressive revellers in heightened mood. *Honeymoon* neatly inscribes the present nature of service station night:

interplay of bodies, shadows; a transit of physical energy and psychic wanderings.

What does this all add up to? Is it just a somnambulist drift through common-places without purpose? Well partly that is the point, to glimpse this world like a moth bumping against the restaurant windows. We have seen actions, reflections and ourselves too. This text has imagined a generic motorway service station where a range of night geographies – for example those of gender, commerce, and community – are played out. We have seen how the flat, blank plan of the building as a diagram of functions, is overwritten by the reality of the motorway service station – a venue of codified and yet unbounded human and commercial interactions.

Through this examination, the spaces have become distinct from everyday commercial space by our discovery of the patina of human activity: metaphorical and physical traces of being. We have seen how the darkness brings light to hidden practices in hidden spaces, and how the geography of the night-time service station is important in the construction of filmic and textual narratives. Finally, we can begin to chart a territory of existence beyond the simple destination, when A to B is not the point.

Now, it's dawn again. The business travellers are pulling in for coffees and croissants, or Fried Chicken breakfasts. The traces of the night are wiped-clean, washed down, erased, but the study of these micro landscapes, and others like them continues, to see what emerges through exploring, understanding and mapping how we behave in these places out of time, after dark.

David Lawrence

Acknowledgements:

Thank you to John Berger; Miranda Bowen; Mary Lunan; ECP Cari Mitchell; Kerri Swindells; Dr Belinda Brooks-Gordon, Manchester Concord Club; Ron Peck; Jeremy Wood.

Endnotes:

[1] For example litter picks.
[2] See George Simmel. *The Metropolis and Mental Life*. p15. http://www.blackwellpublishing.com/content/BPL_Images/Content_store/Sample_chapter/0631225137/Bridge.pdf. (Accessed 1 August 2011).
[3] See Richard Hornsey. *Hornsey, Richard. The Spiv and the Architect: Unruly Life in Postwar London*. Minneapolis; London: University of Minnesota Press, 2010, p90.
[4] John Berger. *The Red Tenda of Bologna*. London: Drawbridge Books, 2007, P. 34. Quoted by kind permission of John Berger.
[5] See http://www.godmanchester.net/images/inn.jpg.
[6] Commercial hospitality companies leased service area sites from the government.
[7] *Edward Hopper* (1981). Directed by Ron Peck (UK).
[8] Iain Sinclair. *London Orbital: A Walk around the M25*. London: Penguin Books: 2003, pp143-44.
[9] See John Berger, *Pig Earth*, Berger, John. *Pig Earth* (first published 1979). London: Bloomsbury, 1999, pxxvi.
[10] Armitage, Simon. *The Motorway Service station as a Destination in its Own Right*. Sheffield: Smith/Doorstop Books, 2009.
[11] *Cantagallo – A BP Film* (c. 1964). Written and directed by Jeff Inman (UK/Italy).
[12] *Hell Drivers* (1957). Directed by C. Raker Endfield (UK).
[13] *The Leather Boys* (1964). Directed by Sidney J. Furie (UK).
[14] Peter L. Cave. *Chopper: England's King of the Angels*. London: New English Library, 1971.
[15] Frank Mort, *Capital Affairs: London and the Making of the Permissive Society*. New Haven & London: Yale University Press, 2010, p213.
[16] *Charlie Bubbles* (1967). Directed by Albert Finney (UK).
[17] Director Ron Peck speaking during his film *Edward Hopper* (1980).
[18] Jim (Ken Robertson) to Judy (Rachel Nichols James) in *Nighthawks* (1978) Directed by Ron Peck assisted by Paul Hallam.
[19] John W. Dagion [ed.]. *Hot Tricks: True Revelations and Strange Happenings from 18 Wheeler*. San Francisco: Leyland Publications, 1989.

[20] For example: boards.gaybod.com/discus/messages/156/5823. htm l?1292269364

[21] *Fling.com* also masquerades as *fbooksluts.com*, and *flirtnaughty.com* is identical to *letsgodogging.com*, down to the page format and the people it suggests are messaging the user. (Some of whom no longer exist as members themselves).

[22] LYMM in particular as it is on the route between the continent and Ireland.

[23] http://www.swingingheaven.co.uk/dogging/locations/cheshire-dogging.html
http://www.dogging.co.uk/forum/dogging-lounge/156356
http://www.localdoggingads.co.uk/dogging.shtml

[24] websites include http://www.gaydar.co.uk.

[25] See: http://www.grindr.com/Grindr_iPhone_App/What_is_Grindr.html

[26] See http://www.manchesterconcord.org.uk/jessica2.htm

Motorway Twitter Poems

Here I am on the tarmac; it is true it bears no message. But on the road, what material for semiology! (Thank you, Roland Barthes)

* * *

I flew over a motorway once. It looked beautiful, bathed in sodium light with the car headlights like stair-rods and the catseyes blinking.

Joe Moran

M62

The highway is often the only thing that moves in some parts of the country. A steady line of lights that illuminate a sullen September night. Moving beacons of desolation carrying people to places that they could not easily have reached 50 years ago.

The separated settlements of the M62 are under threat. The demand for new houses is eating up the fields, because it's cheaper than diversifying into existing urban areas. A gay abandon of cheapness and avarice gives acres of uniformity and boredom across the region. A boredom that underlines a hopelessness of humanity. RESULT – RIOT – done in the name of housing provision – people on housing estates more than 2.5 kilometres from the centre of Barnsley do not belong, or feel they belong, to the town. They live nowhere.

The M62 line contains riots – people who see others with things they do not have – equality of helping yourself, not helping yourself.

A field of homes, reducing the view to a field of homes, with nothing in them, because people have nothing. A view limited by the view.

Belong to something – anything. A hundred cities, towns and villages along the line bound together by a road that empties them.

The middle aged and the youth move out to work and study leaving the elderly to fend for themselves in a sea of emptiness until the itinerants return as they are going to bed.

Dreams have withered on this route. Nothing. Nothing to offer. Nothing doing. A raw canvas of unprimed possibility.

How many businesses could exist along the M62 employing five persons or less? If 15 million people live, coast to coast, along the line, it is reasonable to assume that 6 million work, or at least should be working. Of the 6 million workers there are 20% unemployed.

1.2 million people required to work, approximately 220,000 new small business would render 100% employment. The beauty of the small enterprise is that they do not have to grow. Enough money for a home, holiday and a few treats is a sustainable model for the economy. More importantly, small concerns involve all members of staff in a meaningful way that gives validation to their existence. A sense of responsibility for all ages. Happiness is the root ambition for all, not vast accumulation of wealth at the expense of the unfortunate. No HR department, no Health and Safety, no board meetings. MORE INVENTION AND CREATIVITY!!

The M62 community has choices. For those morning people they can enjoy the sun rising over the North Sea giving hope to the day. Other night creatures watch the sun going down over the Irish Sea preparing them for a nocturnal treat. In between are many other views from the Pennines to the flood plains of the east. 15 million people connected by many views. The importance of the view to a sense of well being is critical to happiness and the east/west line of the highway gives possibility.

The large number of cities, towns, villages and hamlets already give choice, but the demand for new homes, and the earning of planning permissions for green field development which results in vast swathes of nowhere ville, often known as suburbs. The suburban sprawl destroys existing communities and breeds discontent through no sense of place. A house is not a home.

For much of the day the M62 is a car park. Thousands of people staring at a view they did not intend to see. A start of a day they did not intend to have. Many rise in the dark to make the journey before others. No one should rise before the sun. No meaningful train to catch – no alternative. I propose to take cars off the highway and replace them with comfortable and frequent buses which are punctual. One lane in each direction would be reserved for trunks, to keep them off the A and B roads. A series of service stations would be developed as park and ride with useful shopping, cultural and community facilities that would form the new heart of new settlements. People will continue to travel further than they should to work and thus new 'towns' would permit people to rise from their bed at a decent hour, breakfast at home and take their motor car on a short journey to their nearest new park and ride town. On their return they may socialise here before retiring home.

Time is Everything and Routine is Good for the Body

The M62 life means movement of people. It is the modern condition. Movement means travellers' tales. Tales have to be told somewhere. The somewhere must be congenial and appropriate. Where?

The new form of the motorway service area is a major focus for the SuperCity. This is the place where travellers leave their cars after a short B road journey before catching the bus; it is also the place where they transfer at the end of their day. A place to exchange tales of the futility of management, the new lover and the condition of their lives. A place where Manchester stories rub shoulders with Hull reminiscence. A place in which to clear the day's detritus before an evening of leisure (NO OVERTIME IN THE SUPERCITY).

M62

My first trip along the M62 was with Cliff Barnett in a very smart Jaguar from Leeds to Liverpool. We glided past the longest row of terraced houses in the world and lifted up towards the Pennines. Past Halifax, (the 'friend of the motor car'), Italianate Mills, a divided highway which embraces a recalcitrant farmer, until we descend to Northern Edge of Manchester. Warrington with Ikea, the most visited building in the North West, to Liverpool. We sat in St George's Hall and got berated for being architects, even though we had arrived at the city's invitation, made our own left wing cup of tea and fucked off. That was the first time Liverpool was rude to me, but little did I think that 20 years later they would do the same again when they lied to me about the Fourth Grace by suggesting that the people of the city did not like it. In reality they had spent my budget on another project that went well over budget. What I did notice was that the good people that lived there always treated me well and appeared to love the idea of a floating cloud on their waterfront.

The spirit of the people across the whole length of the M62 is extraordinary. They are bound together with a sense of humour, resilience and a lack of expectation that they will ever be treated properly. They are individuals that dare to dream. They can imagine fun, but sadly tend to be let down by their politicians who assume that the 'NORMAL' is safe.

The real population verge on madness, a quality that binds them together and that is why they belong together in one city. A CITY OF SPIRIT.

Will Alsop

Motorway prayer poems

Let us spray

Let us spray
For we know no other way to travel
than the wet road way

Let us spray
Let us aquaplane
Let us thrash our wheels through a wash
of wicked water
Let us squint through a screen of grey

Let us spray
Though we endanger
Our companions on the sluicing skid-surface
Let us spray
between their dazzling foglights
and their indistinct headlights
Let us spray
through the terror of dabbed brakelights
and the torment of the torrent
Let us spray

O blackened cloud protect us
Let us spray
O dreadful deluge purge us
Let us spray
O glassy tarmac shift us
Let us spray

Prayer in the wind

Bless all drivers of high-sided vehicles,
Bless all seagulls blown off course,
Bless all shoppers whose carrier bags are erratic sails in a bad storm.
Bless those who really are at sea, in cavernous calamitous waves.

Bless the blades of the wind turbines,
Bless the shuddering power lines,
Bless the deep roots of tall trees.

Bless the vulnerable heads of baldies,
Bless the knocked knees of pensioners,
Bless the knuckles of straining cyclists.

Bless the high crane operators, the scaffolders, the window-cleaners.
Bless the course of the hopeful spot-kick and the aircraft.

Bless the homeless ones,
Bless the scared ones,
Bless the roof tiles.

Prayer at Junction 38

Bless those who nurse and nurture horticulture:
-the big Van Dijks' expanding their glass avenues to every field's edge;
-the humble Walkers' selling veg from a roadside tin shed;
-the elderly lady at Bridge Farm trimming rose bushes beneath the last eastbound motorway exit sign.

Bless the opportunity seekers and the individual entrepreneurs on the B1230;

-Sunday Car Boot-goers selling and buying in a farmyard by The Mires;
-the man filling a bucket with apples from a tree on the slip road.

Bless the quarry workers and the edible oil recyclers
working from behind security fences and down dusty lanes,
and the drivers of the trucks and carriers which sustain their trade.

Bless the lonely staff police guarding abandoned vehicles
in their compound at the junction of the old redundant road.

Bless the wildfowl and the Sunday twitchers of North Cave Nature Reserve;
the horse-and-carriage leisure takers down Dryham Lane;
the anglers of Newport's generous lakes and canal sides.

At this place of anonymous endings and surprising starts
bless the Hull-bound
and those facing the Pennine haul,
and the staff of The Triangle petrol station serving the needs of them all.

Prayer at Junction 37
Howden to Goole: 11th September 2007

Hail historic Howden huddled in the sun.
Hail the mighty Minster: audaciously lasting and large.
Hail its saints Peter and Paul guarding the West Wall.
Hail John of Howden, each subsequent cleric's local exemplar.
Hail the wood carver Mousy Thomson, and the thirty little mice

he crafted into the Minster's beams.

Hail the cheese shop of Howden and its pavement patrons supping morning coffee;
Hail the sleepy craft shops, the well stocked sweet shops, the high priced hairdressers and fussy boutiques of this holy town.

Hail the Co-op serving all and the Press Association offices bringing the world to Howden and Howden to the world.

Hail the workers of Howden Dyke and Kilpin Pike
-the smartly-dressed Renault mechanics sitting against a wall;
-the staff of the massive Ebuyers shed;
-the dockers, truckers and sewage workers on this wide twist of the River Ouse.

Hail the magnificent M62 as it crosses the Ouse in high style;
Hail the traffic above;
Hail the herons, swans and sheep beneath.

Hail Booth (whoever he was) and his ferry
Hail Boothferry and its bridge

Hail the restless spirits which live directly beneath the M62 Ouse Bridge
unsighted but booming, creaking, groaning
endlessly aching
in the empty concrete vault
above ploughed fields.

Prayer at Junction 34

Thanks for the high places where it is possible to take a long view
-through the long grass,
-over high fields,
of the temporarily tiny towns below.

Thanks for the high places where monuments to human folly:
-pompous pillars ennobling their donors,
-failed mills,
-churches deifying their buried benefactors,
are reduced to scratches and smudges on a vast canvas.

Thanks for the high places where even the random shambles of industrial detritus:
-abandoned works,
-stacked storage units,
-grassed-up quarries and ripped-up concrete yards,
take on shape, pattern, shade and colour.

Thanks for the high places which stop you in your steps,
give cause for reflection,
permit you to turn your back on the rushing traffic,
-to face your Elland, to face your Halifax,
-to face the grass covering your feet,
-to face yourself.

John Davies

Looking for the Linear City

The M62 Motorway has long inspired visions of a resurgent north Joe Moran went to Hull and back in search of it...

'Why don't we cross the city limit and head on down the end of 62?' Liverpool group, It's Immaterial, posed the question on 'Driving away from home,' a haunting road song which was a hit in the summer I sat my O-levels. The chorus warmly recommended driving along the M62 motorway for '30 miles or more' (which seems like a long way when you're 16 and your family doesn't own a car).

Twenty years on, driving along England's only coast-to-coast motorway no longer seems like an alluring alternative to exam revision. When the Queen officially opened the M62 in October 1971, the brochure rashly promised: 'By the mid-1970s, the 130 mile journey from Liverpool to Hull will be cut from five exhausting hours to an easy cruise of less than two hours.' Today it is one of the most congested motorways in the country, without the compensation of being iconically awful like the M25.

Now the M62 is in the vanguard of the movement towards road tolls, made more likely by the Road Transport Bill which gives local councils more power to introduce them in their areas. A recent M62 Route Action Plan, prepared by transport consultancy Halcrow, makes dire predictions about future gridlock if such 'radical measures' are not implemented. The Northern Way, an alliance of regional development agencies aimed at bridging the £30 billion productivity gap between the north and the rest of the country, is lobbying hard among local authorities for M62 tolls, as a way of accelerating both traffic and economic renewal.

Over the last few weeks I have finally taken the song's advice and been driving along the M62. For the Yorkshire poet Simon Armitage, this motorway is like a modern-day Hadrian's Wall, 'a belt drawn tightly across the waistline of Britain, with the buckle somewhere near Leeds'. It marks out the true north, 'where England tucks its shirt in its underpants'. For years the M62 has inspired federalist visions of a growth corridor that would unite the north across the Pennines to form a single entity, like Holland's Randstadt or Germany's Rhine-Ruhr region, and finally challenge the south's economic dominance. The dream has so far been scuppered by, among other things, the tedious reality of the traffic jam. The story of this road, once optimistically named 'the south-east bypass', is also one about the changing idea of motorways in British politics and culture.

In the 1930s, when an east-west coast road was first conceived, Liverpool was at the cutting edge of modern motoring. The East Lancashire Road opened and was meant to run all the way to the Humber – but it got no further than the outskirts of Manchester before the war intruded. It was a sign of Liverpool's long-term decline as a city and port that it was left behind in the first great period of motorway building. The growth in traffic in the 1950s turned the East Lancs Road into a regular bloodbath, until someone had the bright idea of adding a central reservation.

As car ownership spread beyond the middle classes, the first motorways were meant to open up a new, democratic era of mobility and opportunity. When the transport minister, Ernest Marples, officially opened a 72-mile southern stretch of the M1 in November 1959, he hailed a 'magnificent motorway opening up a new era in road travel, in-keeping with the new, exciting, scientific age in which we live'. Pathé newsreels eulogised this 'safe, fast and beautiful' road: 'The great highway will never look empty again. It'll be a crowded road of speed... This is the motoring we used to dream about.' The absence of speed limits on the motorways until 1965, and the fairly light traffic, made them thrilling, glamorous spaces.

Then the dream of the open road slowly soured. The first inkling came with the protests against the urban motorways built in the late 1960s. When Michael Heseltine formally opened London's Westway in July 1970, protestors came armed with placards saying 'You can't fly over human lives' and 'Get us out of this hell'. By October 1986, when she cut the ribbon at the final section of the M25 near Watford, Margaret Thatcher convinced no one when she said that those already moaning about heavy traffic on the road reminded her of the old saying that 'nobody shops at Sainsbury's because of the queues'.

Driving along the M62 today is like reading a primer in this fraught history of British roadbuilding. The road was completed between 1966 and 1976, just as the lustre of the first motorways was wearing off. One consequence, for which Liverpudlians and Hullites should be grateful, is that their towns never became motorway cities like Birmingham or Leeds. The M62 begins a few miles outside Liverpool, in Knotty Ash, and ends several miles from the North Sea, merging anti-climactically into the A63. Around the Greater Manchester and West Yorkshire conurbations it becomes part of a maze-like urban motorway system. But over the Pennines, the road climbs to 1442 feet and becomes quite spectacular, more reminiscent of the straight roads and wide vistas of America and the Continent. The engineers who built this section heroically contended with impassable peat bogs, drifting snow and fierce cross-winds – taming nature for the sake of the car in a way that now seems inconceivable.

On my travels, I hear different versions of the legend of Stott Hall Farm, which stands in the middle of the road as the dual carriageway divides on the Pennine moors. A student working behind the counter at a Caffè Ritazza tells me, with the unshakeable certainty of youth, that the farmer sat on his roof while the motorway was being built around him, trying to drive the workers away by blaring out Led Zeppelin records. The road actually separates for engineering reasons, but people want to believe that the farmer refused to be moved, like a 1970s versions of Swampy – a myth perpetuated in John Shuttleworth's song 'The man who lives on the M62' and numerous hair-raising videos of the farm uploaded onto YouTube, shot by passing drivers from the wheels of their cars.

Why does this nondescript farm inspire such folklore? Perhaps because it stands at a symbolic midway point on the M62, shortly after you see a sign saying 'highest motorway in England'. These 27 miles over the Pennines between Rochdale and Huddersfield have been a mental as well as physical barrier, the foundation for civil wars, sporting rivalries and general bigotry. Such attitudes survive in the people who still talk about 'going over the top' to Yorkshire or Lancashire, as if they are in a war film, or who chant 'Yorkshire sheep shaggers' and 'Wanky-Wanky-Lancashire' at rugby league matches. Rugby league, the second largest spectator sport in Britain, is almost wholly confined to towns along this motorway. A 1994 survey showed that 60 per cent of those regularly attending rugby league matches lived within four postal districts on the M62 corridor. Seen as the quintessentially northern sport, it engenders fierce local feeling and divides the north as much as unites it.

The motorway was supposed to break down these barriers, uniting eastern and western regions with very similar economic and social problems. In the 1970s, local politicians and industrialists came up with a concept known as 'Oceanspan'. Raw materials would arrive from America at Liverpool (traditionally a bulk port), be turned into goods along the manufacturing belt of the M62, and be exported to Europe via the Humber. In the Thatcher era, the regional campaigner David Fletcher founded Transpennine, a thinktank which promoted a similar idea of a 'land bridge' along the M62. The EU then embraced this Transpennine ideal as a way of linking the resurgent Celtic tiger with eastern Europe. The motorway straddles what the EU calls E20, the trade route from Limerick to St Petersburg. Its 1999 European Spatial Development Perspective specifically promotes trading corridors that link ports and join a cluster of cities surrounded by protected countryside – just like the M62.

The New Labour vision of regional devolution latched on to this trans-European strategy. So, in 2004, we had John Prescott's blueprint for a megatropolis running along the M62, inevitably nicknamed 'Prezzagrad'. In the same year, the architect Will Alsop unveiled his still more ambitious plans for a SuperCity, 'Coast to Coast', sited on a

15-mile-wide strip along the length of the motorway. Dismissing the freestanding town as very last century, Alsop dreamed of a 'beautiful urban sprawl' where people would live in Hull, shop in Manchester and work in Liverpool, using an M62 that would no longer carry cars but bullet trains. He cruised along the road in his 4x4 for a Channel 4 series, visions of the future appearing magically in his side window. 15-storey 'city villages' called Stacks, piled high in asymmetrical shapes like chaotic games of Jenga, would 'litter the landscape as objects of curiosity and wonder', he suggested. Alsop mentioned in passing that Liverpool would have to be extended a mile out to sea on stilts, and the centre of Bradford flooded to create a northern Venice.

Will this Xanadu-like vision of regional renewal ever come to pass? The good news is that the privatised Hull and Liverpool ports are doing better business than ever, helped by the accession of eastern European states into the EU. And the expansion of the John Lennon Airport has also led to a growth in traffic between Manchester and Liverpool, including the dinky blue airport bus that I overtake several times on my journeys. But the linear city of 'LiverHull' remains elusive. A few years ago the traffic consultancy MVA analysed M62 drivers' 'desire lines' – a strangely poetic name for the routes they take on their mundane daily journeys. The map of these desire lines showed the vast majority ending abruptly on either side of the Pennines.

In all my stops on the motorway I cannot find anyone who is going the whole way along it. Desire lines are short and sweet. A man with his two teenage daughters going to the Xscape leisure complex at Castleford; a middle-aged couple from Oldham visiting their grown-up daughter in Leeds; a young woman stopping off at Burtonwood services on her way back from IKEA. Alsop's vision of a strip city has passed them by. Presumably some lorry drivers are going all the way, but they are not refilling in the Moto service station cafes where 'good food is a joy' but a baked potato with beans costs £3.99.

Driving along the M62, you still encounter two separate norths, virtual mirror images of each other. At each end of the motorway there are the flatlands of west Lancashire, where the road is bumpy from mining subsidence, and Yorkshire's East Riding, where it is surrounded by recently-closed collieries. And on either side of the Pennines is the classic northern industrial landscape of old textile mills, redundant chimneys and rows of aged terraced housing. A 2001 study by the University of Birmingham's Centre for Urban and Regional Studies found that 280,000 homes along the M62 corridor (16.3% of the total) were abandoned, obsolete or affected by low demand. This study inspired the establishment of the nine 'pathfinder' housing renewal areas, six of which straddle the corridor.

You get a dramatic lesson in this brutal economic geography simply by driving along the M62. At the eastern and western edges of the motorway, at least outside of rush hour, the traffic is sparse. You are bumbling along the inside lane of a nearly deserted highway when, around the main junctions with the M6, M1 and A1, you encounter a swarm of cars, cutting you up with death-defying lane changes. If the traffic flows are anything to go by, the M62 seems to have perpetuated the economic dominance of Manchester and Leeds rather than achieve its original aim, which was to spread wealth to the edges.

The Pennines used to be the 'lungs of England', a weekend playground for Lancashire and Yorkshire's millworkers. Now the M62 is another sort of playground – of reservoirs given over to powerboating and windsurfing, and indoor leisure hangars with snow slopes, rock climbing and skating rinks. All the towns along the motorway are competing with one another over what seem like very similar attractions, trying to get you to turn off to visit their retail or entertainment experience. The only towns that don't clamour for attention like this are Leeds and Manchester – because they don't have to. If you were a foreign tourist travelling on the M62, judging the area solely by its tourist signs, you might think that Pontefract was the booming capital of Yorkshire and Leeds a suburban backwater.

Up until now this is what motorways have been like: semi-autonomous, micro-societies in which the outside world is signposted but rarely encountered. As the novelist J.G. Ballard once wrote, British motorway drivers have become 'citizens of a virtual city-state borne on a rush of radial tyres'. Finally, though, we are learning to accept that access to roads is an expensive and scarce commodity. Most of the drivers I encountered at M62 service stations saw road tolls as inevitable, and were more concerned with the practicalities of running and policing them than with the much-vaunted 'war on the motorist'. And tolls may not simply be a way of cutting congestion but of linking motorways with the towns through which they pass – perhaps finally creating the lost city of LiverHull along the roadside.

Joe Moran

Soft Estate

Because they are rarely seen statically, roadscapes undermine our Ruskinian ideal of landscape as a view seen at once from a privileged vantage point by a single viewer... our culture has learnt to interpret landscapes in a particular way – to read water meadows as picturesque, mountains as rugged or fenland as inscrutable. But we haven't been taught to read roadscapes, because they seem too mundane and too fleetingly viewed to form any part of any imagined ideal. In order to make sense of them, we need to re-educate our eyes. Joe Moran[1]

Soft Estate is the term used by the Highways Agency to describe the grass verges and other natural habitats that line our motorways and trunk roads (some 30,000 hectares of land nationally). Whilst roads play a major role in opening up land for access and development, their attendant verges offer a genuine refuge for wildlife and a metaphorical wilderness in the midst of intense urbanisation. These peripheral and largely unrecorded landscapes correspond to what Ignassi de Solà-Morales Rubió called *'Terraine Vague'*, areas of 'unincorporated margins, interior islands void of activity, oversights, these areas are simply *uninhabited, un-safe, un-productive...* and in terms of what they represent, ...as much a critique as a possible alternative'.[2]

I began making paintings and other related works exploring these *edgeland* road sites several years ago because it became increasingly apparent on my regular journeys from London to Canterbury that here was a landscape full of contradictions: a threshold environment where agriculture collides with urbanisation; wild seeds blow down asphalt arteries; stems of yellow ragwort stealthily encroach on Moto car parks and the relentless din of artic trucks drowns the buzz and clicks of insects. Here was a world of contested values, already in the first bloom of economic and environmental degeneration, usually seen from the bubble of a vehicle but thrown into a headlight magnifier lens of increased amplitudes when accessed on foot.

These territories represented the culturally soporific but environmentally acute: ripe for aesthetic analysis and historical contextualisation. Politics is embedded in our landscape through histories of enclosure and ownership. The new roads that make land accessible for development also close it off to the public. Land where people once walked freely is sliced away and, in a latter-day kind of enclosure, pedestrians are now forbidden. The discourses around these borderlands seemed rich for exposure and representation. Often ignored, untouched and usually unprotected, these spaces represent a new kind of frontier with an emergent sense of uniqueness.

While early tourists travelled to areas such as The Lakes to capture images of wild places, in today's countryside uncontrolled wilderness springs up in the margins of our transport networks and the semi-derelict grid plans of industrialised corridors. These spaces, aptly described in Paul Farley and Michael Symmons-Roberts' book *Edgelands: Journeys into England's True Wilderness*, form a truer picture of our experience of landscape than we might care to imagine.[3]

Our strategically marketed National Parks and rural meadows are laden with contrary expectations. Road journeys often frame and inform these expectations. Photographer Fay Godwin described being 'lured into the countryside, only to find most of it out of bounds, while we are fobbed off with substitutes like country parks and theme parks'.[4]

Eighteenth Century tourists accessed these new territories equipped with a Claude Glass. Today's traveller might see the equivalent in the gentle convex curvature of the rear view mirror as the landscape rapidly recedes then dissolves. Modern motorway design incorporates 'Clothoid' or transition curves, features that focus drivers' attention so that they stay alert. These have the effect of smoothing the landscape reminiscent of Eighteenth Century parks, where curved carriage drives managed the experience of the landscape. Motorways arguably represent the modern equivalent of the spectacular re-sculpting of the landscape undertaken by designers such as by Capability Brown.

'Re-educating our eyes'? At first sight, highways appear inert, empty places, devoid of any meaning or value. They are places we 'see' constantly

as we travel around but in which we do not invest cultural value or our aesthetic regard. But on closer inspection, the wealth of unusual visual detail and strange nuances of light within their fabric often provides visual splendour. This narrow ribbon of land acts as both a frame and barrier to the vistas behind.

Quite apart from the fact that these sites are not systematically documented through their changing development, when they do have visual representation this is nearly always in film (e.g. the genre of the 'road movie') or from the standpoint of 'motion', through the car window, nearly always seen at distance, unreachable and in motion. Photographed in the works of artists like Andrew Cross or Andreas Gursky, they are rarely recorded through painting.

For me, questions arise from how 'still' and yet *'elaborated'*[5] paintings can develop from drawings, dispassionate documentary photographic sources and from the tropes of moving road film imagery: how something usually experienced either moving and with shifting parallax or conversely with snapshot brevity might be experienced as a 'still' but 'continuous' image. In this sense, a film such as Patrick Keiller's *Robinson in Ruins* exploring such sites with its use of *moving stills* might be experienced in a similar way to painting.

Culturally what does the act of painting or representing a photographic image in paint bring to our reading of or understanding of that image, and particularly our 'reading' of these particular landscapes? Arguably, painting invests cultural value and emotional significance in images that in photographic form might be deadpan and forensic.

Historical

Major roads have rarely escaped political association. The large roads built by General Wade into Scotland following the 1715 Scottish Jacobite uprising provided the access for Paul Sandby's topographical and cartographic depiction of Scottish land handed to its new 'English' owners. This road building paved the way for a host of 'picturesque' tourists. In depicting idealised country seats and associated land, Sandby was also depicting the established social order – using the recognised structure of 'owner' portrait set against backdrop of land owned.

These insular and stately environments provided the experimental and political backdrop to the early English Landscape tradition. Lancelot 'Capability' Brown fashioned landscapes for this set of land owning classes whose estates were artificially rusticated and re-set according to paradigms from classical painters such as Claude Lorraine and associated classical literature. Crucially, many of the 'viewing stations' spread around these large estates were to be seen from the privileged viewpoints of horseback or carriage whilst in motion. Arboreta normally had 'rides' and the whole was intended to be experienced as a kind of moving stage set. Idealised capriccio, Arcadian follies and related buildings would have sudden and surprising new 'reveals' as paths wove between artificial coppice and parkland and the parallax defined the space.

Similarly, as we drive, our relationship to the sculpted ravines of motorway gorges, sudden lateral views and bridges changes; different vistas open out and suddenly shut down as we move through the landscape in a speeded up way. Interrupt this commonplace visual experience by freezing a glance and you might give people a kind of laterally viewed clip of a landscape, normally encountered in milliseconds.

When the M1 was originally built, the chief architect Owen Williams, began to worry about the soporific effects of straight lines and started to introduce what is known as the 'transition' or 'Clothoid' curve, a gently accelerating arc that gradually slows momentum as well as sustaining the driver's attention. Originally developed by a Devon County surveyor, Henry Criswell in 1937, Williams took this further, sending his son, Owen T. Williams to study Robert Moses' suburban parkways in New York, whose meandering paths borrowed much from Eighteenth Century English landscape gardens that were diametrically opposed to the French grids.[6] These inclines, gorges and curves give credence to Carl Andre's idea of British landscape already being 'one vast earthwork'[7] and Lancashire's motorway engineer James Drake believing roads should be 'sculpture on an exciting, grand scale, carving, moulding and adapting... earth, rock, and minerals into a finished product which must be both functional *and pleasing to the eye'.*[8]

Here we have the Twentieth Century revved up equivalent of the country park, viewed at speed but with all the attendant banks and escarpments. William Gilpin once described Lakeland views from a carriage window seen in a Claude glass as 'a succession of high coloured pictures... continually gliding before the eye'. Already landscape has been both framed and possessed.[9]

Ultimately the dislocation and 'prising away of life from place, an abstraction of experience into different kinds of touchlessness'[10] throws up a tension between the experience of sublimity that is heightened through motion, expanse and repetition and views which can, in some cases, be possessed.

Political

The depiction of landscape topography and the picturesque has strong roots in ideas about ownership. Uncontained, natural wilderness however, came to represent lack of control, lack of agency and with the terrible diminution experienced – obscurity.[11] This flew against the control and order of the picturesque often 'determined by an excess of form'.[12] A passage in Jane Austen's *Northanger Abbey* wryly suggests how these tasteful forms masked political sensitivities such as the Enclosure Act.[13]

Motorway *Soft Estate* environments are controlled, manufactured and yet wild – qualities simultaneously like formal gardens and bunker shaped moraines. Like a latter day kind of enclosure, their very inaccessibility hints at the power of The State. Yet they are susceptible to contrary subliminal readings – lack of boundaries, trespass and unfettered nature. These verges are restricted places. We are forbidden to stop on the motorway unless we break down. Access to them is strictly controlled and often monitored by remote cameras. Like J. G. Ballard's *Concrete Island*, the verge is a metaphor for something forbidden and inaccessible, and once there, almost inescapable.

These 'Island' hyper-landscapes contain worlds in which our rapid through-transit alters our sense of scale, which is simultaneously diminished and increased. These are fragile, yet extremely self-sustaining and hard environments, changing landscapes embodying both beauty and survival.

Artist Richard Long's professed antagonism to land ownership and to capital finds a simple outlet in that most democratic means of transport and viewing the landscape – walking.[14] It is, somewhat perversely only through walking that these road landscapes can be accessed and closely encountered. Accessing these environments embodies all the sensations of trespass and in accessing them by foot there are connections with 'the right to roam'. Trespassing events, such as the mass trespass on Kinder Scout moors in 1932, are again coming under legislative pressure with legal means at the disposal of landowners and managers such as 'aggravated trespass'.

Writer and environmental campaigner, Marion Shoard describes these areas as 'raw and rough, and rather than seeming people-friendly are often sombre and menacing, flaunting their participation in activities we do not wholly understand. They certainly do not conform to people's idea of the picturesque by presenting a chocolate-box image, suitably composed and textural. On the contrary, they seem desolate, forsaken and unconnected even to their own elements let alone to our preferred version of human life.'[15] We often pass them by. Again as Shoard has suggested, 'we may not notice it, but it is here that much of our current environmental change… is taking place' in spite of which 'edgelands have become the lowest grade of landscape in UK landscape conservation terms'.[16]

Celebrating these sometimes spectacular places is nevertheless tinged with unease because of the uncertain nature of their existence and the environmental questions they pose.

I would agree with Shoard's assertion that, 'it is time for the edgelands to get the recognition that Emily Brontë and William Wordsworth brought to the moors and mountains and John Betjeman to the suburbs. They too have their story. It is the more cogent and urgent for being the story of our age.'[17]

Edward Chell

Endnotes:

[1] Moran, J. *'On Roads. A Recent History'* published by Profile Books, London, 2009. p148.

[2] *Terrain Vague* by Ignasi de Solà-Morales Rubió. From Davidson, C. *Anyplace*, MIT Press, Cambridge, Massachussettes, USA. 1995. pp118 – 123.

[3] Farley, Paul & Symmons-Roberts, Michael. *Edgelands: Journeys Into England's True Wilderness* published by Jonathan Cape, London. 2011 – pp 100 – 101.

[4] Godwin, F. *'Our Forbidden Land'* published by Jonathan Cape, London. 1990. p23.

[5] 'Whereas a painting needs to *elaborate* work to render it realist, a documentary requires self-conscious stylisation if it is not to appear realistic.' Panse, S. 'The Film-maker as *Rückenfigur.* Documentary as Painting in Alexandr Sokurov's *Elegy of a Voyage.*' *Third Text*, Vol 20, Issue 1, January 2006, p13.

[6] *op cit.,* Moran. pp.32 – 34

[7] Andrews, M. *'Landscape and Western Art'* published by Oxford University Press, 1999. p215

[8] *op cit.,* Moran. p34

[9] *op cit.*, Andrews. p116

[10] Macfarlane, R. *Walking the walk, talking the talk'* p163. *The Wild Places*, published by Granta, London. p203

[11] The obscurity described by Burke had several causes, one of which came out of succession and repetition. The artificial infinity of the modern day verge – with its soporific rhythms of posts, markers and flyovers has an equivalence here.

> 'Succession and *uniformity* of parts, are what constitute the artificial infinite. 1. *Succession*; which is requisite that the parts may be continued so long and in such a direction, as by their frequent impulses on the sense to impress the imagination with an idea of their progress beyond their actual limits. 2. *Uniformity*; because if the figures of the parts should be changed, the imagination at every change finds a check; you are presented at every alteration with the termination of one idea, and the beginning of another; by which means it becomes impossible to continue the uninterrupted progression, which alone can stamp on bounded objects the character of infinity. It is in this kind of artificial infinity...the imagination has no rest.'

Burke, Edmund. *A philosophical Enquiry into the Origin of our Ideas of the Sublime and the Beautiful.* Third Edition. Published London, 1761. pp132 – 133.(Sect IX on *Succession & Uniformity*) See also p138 (Sect X1 on *Infinity*) and p144. (Sect XV on *Light*)

[12] Hazlitt, William. (1778 – 1830) *On the Picturesque and the Ideal, a Fragment.* See eds. Harrison, C. Wood, P & Gaiger, J. *Art in Theory 1815 –1900.* published 1998 by Blackwell, p114

[13] Austen, Jane. Northanger Abbey. See Oxford University Press World Classic edition, 1972. p116

[14] *op cit.*, Andrews. p215 – 216.

[15] Shoard, Marion. *Edgelands: Remaking the Landscape* published by Profile Books. 2002. See http://www.marionshoard.co.uk/Documents/Articles/Environment/Edgelands-Remaking-the-Landscape.pdf

[16] *op cit.*, Shoard, M

[17] *op cit.*, Shoard, M

Route Recalculation

England's motorways run
river like coast to coast

All roads lead north

where the heart remains
unappreciated

Occasionally we meander
like a tributary

Through dark mist shrouded
lanes and for an instant
like granules in a jar

I settle

Andrew Taylor

A Proposal

Title of work: **The Islington Radial**

Location: Islington, Liverpool next to the Wellington Column, William Brown Street.

About Liverpool: Liverpool, mighty metropolis on the River Mersey, former gateway for millions of immigrants and emigrants, is both at the end and the beginning of the line. It is the terminus and start of the Trans Pennine Express train route that heads from Liverpool through Manchester, Huddersfield, Leeds and onto Hull, following the trajectory of the M62. Liverpool is also the starting/finishing point of the Leeds-Liverpool Canal that runs for 127 miles, again across the Pennines, through Bootle, Melling, Burscough, Wigan, Blackburn, Burnley, Skipton and Saltaire onto Leeds; and the East Lancashire Road from Liverpool to Manchester. It was supposed to be the start and finish of the M62 motorway.

Description of the work:

Mechanical reproduction emancipates the work of art from its parasitical dependence on ritual. To an even greater degree the work of art reproduced becomes the work of art designed for reproducibility – Walter Benjamin.

Art in the street? Why not?! But only if it is rethought, revised and re-orientated. It would be a mistake to suggest that there is a kind of equality between the museum and the street. They have little in common. And a lot of differences... The point is that the unlimited freedom given to the artist in the museum no longer obtains in the street... The point is that in the city, politics and economics are involved in everything – Daniel Buren.

The Islington Radial is a traditional piece of public art. This 18 foot high piece is a hand-carved white marble sculpture of a pigeon. This matches in size, the Liver Birds that perch on the Royal Liver Building. The sculpture is housed on a three tier square pedestal similar to that of its near neighbour, Wellington's Column.

It is important to note that this is a pigeon not a dove. The often maligned pigeon is a common feature of most cities and it is this fact that forms part of the resonance of the piece, alongside the sculpture's colour – the white pigeon often being mistaken as a dove, the symbol of peace.

Islington, was to be the probable terminus of the M62 motorway in Liverpool. The Inner Liverpool Motorway (ILM) would have been a massive undertaking sweeping around the city, from Islington, rather like the M8 in Glasgow.

The rival cities of Liverpool and Manchester would have been forever linked not only by the Manchester ship canal and the East Lancashire Road, but the M62, the M602 and the ILM. The plan for this link was scrapped after the Shankland Report of 1962.

The Islington Radial celebrates the link between these two great cities and seeks to reaffirm the bond between them. In these days of petty rivalries perpetuated by the media, *The Islington Radial* wishes to shift the focus back to when the cities' musical heritage was shared by the likes of Factory Records (Manchester) and Zoo Records (Liverpool). The two cities shared great music venues like The Factory (Manchester) and Eric's (Liverpool) and bands from Manchester such as Joy Division played Eric's and Liverpool bands such as Echo and the Bunnymen would play the Factory.

The domesticated or homing pigeon can travel many miles. During research it has been noted that the Islington Radial as named and shown on the original plans and drawings, resembled somewhat, a bird. Hence the idea of a bird for the sculpture and it seems somewhat prudent for that bird to be a pigeon.

A celebratory plaque should be placed on the mount of *The Islington Radial* taking the opportunity to encompass the new with the traditional aspect of the sculpture. The original motorway sign graphic designers, Jock Kinneir and Margaret Calvert were seen as cutting edge with their deployment of innovative typography and colour palette. This updated version of the sign should be seen as a homage to Kinneir and Calvert with the following text:

The Islington Radial
The M62 Motorway would and should have ended here

The positioning and location of *The Islington Radial* is important.

The bird is to be faced up Islington, eyeing the route where the M62 would have terminated from its journey across the Pennines through Manchester.

Liverpool poet Andrew Taylor has written a poem about *The Islington Radial*. Taylor's interest in public art stems from being poet-in-resident at Liverpool Architecture and Design Trust (LADT). The poem to be situated immediately to the west of the sculpture, and deliberately fixed to the York stone paving with semi-permanent vinyl lettering, reads:

The Lingering Scent of the North

As old as light from stars
these routes map connections

across hills down urban
corridors until they hit water

like de-freezered ice-cream river
mist rises hiding the source

of a tolling bell a building
shaped like a ship's bow contains

memories of room service and to think
the Liverpool Inner Motorway

would have followed the curvature
past dock walls up north past suburbia

and out back past points of departure
the lights thin the air becomes

cooler and somehow homing pigeons
know to return

Andrew Taylor

Homes not Roads

There were many swarms this summer, the bee man told her, squinting out across the valley as though scanning the horizon for more. "It's the works they're doing, the road building." They stood with the sun on their faces and looked across the fields to the great hills that marched westwards into the distance. And then she heard it rising up from far below; a faint grinding noise, the chewing and scraping of some mournful beast.

"There you are," the bee man nodded. "They're ripping out the woods along the bottom of the valley, all the hollow trunks are going. Nowhere left for the bees to nest you see. This is what you get."

The swarm had appeared that morning, dangling from the eaves of the guest barn like a seething, velvety fruit. She'd heard the children shouting and found Tess trying to poke it with a broom handle. Bruno wanted to stroke it.

"What do you do up here then?" The bee man sounded amused and a little suspicious. Maybe that was the accent. Being older, his was quite strong. She'd forgotten his name already. Pete, Phil?

"Well, it's a sort of treatment, therapy retreat." She felt so awkward when local people asked that question. Couldn't find an answer that sounded right.

"You get people turning up in some pretty smart cars." He raised an eyebrow and his face creased into a quizzical smile. "Some chap in a Porsche stopped at the pub and asked the way here."

"Yes we have corporate groups, teambuilding, and people who just want to get away and reconnect with..." she trailed off.

"They don't mind roughing it then? A sort of yuppie Butlins!" He chuckled to himself.

She folded her arms and tried to smile. "Well not quite!" She blustered. "Some of them are important, you know demanding jobs. They just need a different kind of break."

"Yes of course." He looked at the ground, realising he'd nettled her.

Funny farm the locals called it. The couple they'd got in to help clean and garden used to say that – not to her face of course. That was in the early days when she and David thought they could afford staff. Now all the work was down to them.

There was a shout. David was coming across the paddock, picking his way barefoot through the anthills and thistles, waving at them to hurry up. "I've got clients arriving this afternoon," he called as he got closer. "From *London*."

Silence.

"Darling, this is Pete, sorry, Phil, I don't think you've met. He was just telling me what a busy time…"

"No, no," David shut his eyes and shook his head. "Jess, sweetheart, I don't think you realise quite how serious…" He spoke through gritted teeth in his calm-but-might-loose-it voice. "The sodding thing looks like it's going to fall on someone's head." He covered his face with his hands for a moment, then turned to the bee man. "Look, it's this way, follow me."

She watched them head towards the guest barn. David, tall and angular, stumbling on the uneven ground. The bee man with his slightly stumpy legs, rolling smoothly along beside him. Was it Phil or Pete? Well, at least she'd managed to find him, after a frantic forty minutes going through the Yellow Pages. It turned out he only lived down the lane.

There was so much to do, she felt unable to move. Chore paralysis.

Crickets clicked all around her in the so-called paddock – it was riddled with ant hills – hundreds of them. Earthy domes, mostly deserted and sprouting grass like the heads of some buried army, lost on the Ridgeway. The villagers had a good snigger about that too. Knowing how much they'd paid for the place, people liked to tell them they'd been fleeced. *That paddock would kill a horse. Nice view, shame about that pile of stones. Best pull it down and start again.* But she sensed envy in their laughter. And fascination.

The farmhouse was ancient. It crouched on the brow of the hill, like a sentinel, gazing out over the tops of the downs. Well Farm. Near the crossroads, on Gibbet Hill. Lots of people were buried up here. In the bumps and mounds on the crest of the hill. And in the ditch along their boundary, the old farmer had found the skeleton of a young woman. So they said.

The contours of an Iron Age fort rippled in the field beyond their land. The farmhouse stood on the site of an ancient watering hole for people travelling the Ridgeway. She half closed her eyes and pictured the people who would have stopped here, thousands of them over the years. Traders, soldiers, pilgrims and priests. It would have been a sort of Iron Age Travelodge.

The faint chewing of the bulldozers in the valley below was pierced by a sharp howl and she saw David run from the guest barn towards the house. Oh God, had he been stung? Or the children? She had no idea where they were playing. Sudden images of the uncovered well flashed through her as she pounded across the paddock, but then she saw a silver convertible, bumping up the track and heard David yelling in her direction, "Carnts, Carnts!" What was he saying? "Clients! The fucking clients are early!" He stopped in the herb garden, smoothed his hair and darted round to the front of the house to greet them.

* * *

She found the well cover fixed securely in place. Relief tinged with guilt washed over her. The children were nearby collecting worms from the compost bin. Bruno had filled his beach bucket with squirmy spaghetti. Tess lined them up on the path. "It's a café for birds," she announced. "Amazing darling!"

The bee man gave her a nod as he skirted round the raised beds, back to his car carrying a large white box – presumably with the swarm in it. She hoped David would have the sense to get the new arrivals chatting to him – real life country person. That would buy them ten minutes to get things under control.

Oh God, the clients, the clients. There were six this weekend; a full house for the sweat lodge and shamanic healing package. That's what David had scrawled on his whiteboard. And FLEETWIND. That must be the shaman he'd booked to lead it.

As she dived into the kitchen through the back door, she saw three men in expensive casual clothing were already wielding axes over by the woodpile. Having set them to work, David chivvied and cheered them on. "Nice work, great stuff," as he gathered logs in a barrow and ferried them to the sweat lodge in the small wood.

David could have bought logs ready chopped to size, but this was what people were paying for. Hands on. Getting dirty. Getting real.

"Hey guys, I'm gonna need some help – could one of you give me a hand?" David's voice was brisk and upbeat now, scout masterish with a hint of Australian. The tall one, in chinos, and pink polo shirt followed him to the tepee circle in the wildflower meadow.

She washed up, watching the new arrivals through the open window, wondering what needs and wants they brought with them. They were friends who worked together – something in finance – booked through one of David's old marketing contacts.

David dragged the carpets out of the big tepee – and started beating the woodlice out of them. Jake took his shades off and got going on the sheepskin rugs, thrashing them with a big stick and draping them over the fence. Marriage problems she guessed.

The other two men were still hacking away at the logs. One was jowly, had the look of a heavy drinker. He was wearing suit trousers, with deck shoes, and a rugby shirt – no socks. Still takes his laundry home to mum. Probably has coke in his wash bag. Those types often got tearful and wanted to sit in the kitchen and talk to her late at night.

His friend was in trainers and long shorts. She couldn't make him out at all. He had a thin straight mouth and wore several signet rings and a chunky Rolex. He sat down on a log, lit a cigarette, and scratched his legs. He had incredibly hairy shins. A shape shifter – part frog, part wolf. He'll be the one that complains about them not having a power shower.

It was dark and hot in the kitchen. The Aga blasted out a thick, suffocating heat and the low ceiling and stone flagged floor wrapped around her like the walls of a cave. John Major droned on the radio. A fly buzzed about as she tore open packs of diced meat. Pork casserole and vegetable gratin. Please God none of the clients would look in the bin and see the packaging. With money so tight she'd resorted to cut-price meat. Gloopy pork, exuding pink slime. Basics this, basics that. Well, they were supposed to be reconnecting with the basics – if she threw enough spices in, tinned tomatoes. She sniffed an old pot of cream from the back of the fridge, hesitated, then poured it in.

David bustled in and put the kettle on. He was wearing the T shirt he'd got on his first meditation retreat. That was four years ago now, pre kids, pre country, when they had their London jobs. It was not long after Black Monday. Contracts were drying up. The boom times were over. He'd come back with the idea for this place, a way out of the city, a way forward for them both. The T shirt looked tatty now, but he still liked to wear it for good luck when a new group arrived. It said *connect with the stillness within*.

"They had lunch on the motorway." He filled the cafetiere and added cups and saucers to the big tray. "Set off early. Something about a road protest on the news, thought they'd get held up but no probs. The others are following."

He was calmer now, almost cheerful, which made her feel more panicky.

"Why are they here?" She asked.

"Didn't I tell you?" He rootled in the cupboard by the fridge. "Their friend died in a smash last year. On the M3. Not far from here. Sweetheart where's the tin with the good biscuits, the lemony ones? Ah, yes, here they are!"

"In a car crash?"

"Yes, it's the anniversary. I think they left some flowers at the spot, on the way down here. Darling could you just hold the door open for me?"

The men gathered round the outside table and drank their coffee in the dappled sunlight. She felt sorry for her mean-spirited thoughts. It was a bad habit, sticking people in boxes and laughing at them. Her stupid way of trying to cope. They must have loved their friend. After the initial burst of purposeful activity, they looked crumpled and helpless.

The smoker lit up again and fiddled with his Rolex. The jowly one shrank into the shade, like a forlorn panda pining for home. A few chickens meandered on to the patio and pecked at the biscuit crumbs around their feet, but they didn't notice.

They hunched forwards as David explained the programme. Afternoon meditation in the big tepee followed by supper out in the meadow. At dusk the sweat lodge would be ready and Fleetwind would join them to lead the session. Anyone who wanted to could pick a small tepee and sleep out under the stars.

David leant back and gestured in expansive mode. It amazed her how he could rein in his mood swings and assume this professional persona when he needed to. The children wandered over looking for a biscuit. He made a point of smiling indulgently and introducing them to the clients.

At the beginning they'd talked about family life being at the heart of the business concept. Spiritual retreats in a domestic setting, a rural idyll that offered a model of the work-life balance their target clients craved. That was how they pitched it to the bank. Homestead was a buzz word in their business plan. And spirit work.

They'd talked about moving to the country as though they were planning a holiday. David would handle the client interface while she ran the house. Perfect! And now she looked at these frazzled city workers with envy. They came here to get away from it all and then they went back.

She wanted to ask them, what's so bad about the office? Because she realised now that she'd always quite liked her job. She couldn't remember what was wrong with it.

She shoved the casserole in the Aga and eyed the clock. There were beds to make, toilets to scrub, children's toys to be scrabbled into boxes on hands and knees. Sore hands. Stiff knees. Dry skin. Chipped nails. Festering piles of laundry. Weeds smothering the vegetable garden. Chickens to clean out. And that bloody goat needed milking – if it hadn't already died of mastitis. The reek of it made her want to gag. Every single bloody activity was so labour intensive – even buying a pint of milk meant getting the children into the car and driving a couple of miles.

Tess was talking in a whiny voice. *More* biscuits. David's smile became fixed and started to fade. Bruno's nappy was so full of pee, it sagged, about to fall off. The hens swarmed around his little bucket and knocked it over, pecking at the worms in a frenzy. As the wailing started she realised the children hadn't even had lunch.

Suddenly David sprang up, grabbed a child under each arm, and pitched towards the house like a rugby forward running for a try. He was grim-faced, desperate.

"Why can't you? This… isn't… helping, just keep them out of the way?"

Bruno pawed at her top, "Numnum" he pleaded, nuzzling into her armpit.

"No darling, that's finished, all gone." She tried to sound calm but a dark, acrid fury swelled up in her throat, choking her with the taste of smouldering plastic

She longed to be invisible and far away.

She plonked the children in front of a video with a packet of Cheddars and beakers of squash. Dumbo, that would buy her sixty six minutes, according to the box.

She caught her breath and started lugging the clients' bags from the hall out to the guest barn.

And then she remembered a time last summer when she was driving home from Winchester and they'd closed the motorway because of a smash. It happened just ahead of them. Everything stopped. Engines off. It was so hot that day she got the children out of the car and they sat on the verge with the long grass and cow parsley swaying around them while the air ambulance came and went.

* * *

By the time Fleetwind came zooming up the track in his battered Nissan Micra, the clients had been fed, the children were in bed, asleep.

"Cool place!" He had doeish eyes and long wavy brown hair. He was late.

"David thought you weren't coming."

"Er yeah, there was a problem. This protest, you know they've closed some of the roads."

She led him through the small wood to the sweat lodge. A luminous midsummer sky arched overhead. Wood smoke swirled from the tin chimney and firelight glimmered through the sides of the felted tent. Inside the group was drumming softly as David spoke.

"Working in partnership with the spirits, going through your own enlightenment," his voice was urgent, intense, much deeper than usual. "It's a huge work you know, going into the deepest resources within your self, and removing all obstacles."

She had tried so hard to believe in David's spirit work. It meant so much to him. When they started out she thought it would grow on her. Or that he would grow out of it. There was something so self-indulgent, so navel gazing about it.

Fleetwind's voice, reedy and soporific, rose above the drumming. "The ego wants to ride on the genius of the spirit. It's not our genius that comes through the work of the shaman. You're going for your own enlightenment, your own awakening."

She sighed and looked back at the farmhouse as it hunkered deep into its hollow. The long, stone-tiled roof came down low over the windows, like a battered grey helmet. The windows blinked back the gilded evening sunlight. The house was watchful.

The light would last another hour or so. The children were fast asleep. They wouldn't miss her. She walked away from the house and slipped under the fence into the neighbouring field. The bumps and ridges of the old hill fort stood out starkly in the low sunlight. A fine network of paths and tracks criss-crossed the field. The chain of hills swelled up, then rose and fell in darkening purples and blues as they writhed off into the distance. She could see it now, the dragon's back!

The path that led down into the valley was unfamiliar. She drove everywhere these days – couldn't bring the buggy down a steep track like this. It forked into woodland then passed some farm workers houses where she stopped to catch her breath. Ugly red brick. A man in a camouflage jacket stood in front of one, his hands on his hips.

"Evening". The voice was familiar, but it took her a second to realise it was the bee man. She'd pictured him in an old cottage, small, but not grim like this. The houses on either side of his were boarded up. People had splashed slogans across the walls, in big dripping letters.

Homes not Roads! Motorway Madness! Earthrape!

"Out for a stroll?" He didn't seem particularly pleased to see her. She wondered if they should have paid him for taking the swarm.

There were vehicles all around, clapped out campervans and a pickup truck. Several dogs barked out of sight. The boarded up places appeared to be squatted. There were sheets of corrugated iron, gardening tools and children's toys scattered in the gardens.

"Is it coming this close?"

"The road?" He laughed grimly and rolled his eyes as if to say, where have *you* been?

Of course they knew about the motorway plans when they bought Well Farm. It had been rumbling on for years, the public enquiries and legal challenges. The campaigners used to call at the farm, inviting them to meetings and she would have gone, but David wanted to stay out it. Didn't want to get caught up in the politics, the negative energy. If you show an interest, they'll never leave you alone. You'll get sucked in. They can fight all they like, David said, but they won't stop it. And besides they wouldn't actually see it from the farmhouse.

"They want to blast a cutting through the hill here, take the motorway through the downs."

He gestured towards the fields just beyond the hill fort.

"They say they'll relocate us, but we don't want to go. We'd end up in some poxy estate on the edge of town."

"Alright Dad?" A young man with spiky hair and nose studs came out of the house. An Alsatian rushed out after him and jumped up, pawing her chest and slobbering in her face.

"Calm down Cindy!" The son wrinkled his nose and nodded hello. "That-a-way girl." He threw a stick and the dog plunged into the woods below.

"The road works are further down. We're going there now."

"Will you take me there?" she blurted.

The men looked at each other and shrugged. She could see they didn't want her tagging along.

The son sighed. "You can carry this for us then," he said passing her a big canvas bag. It was heavy. The strap cut into her shoulder. And now she wondered if she really should go. It was too late.

The men tramped ahead of her whacking at brambles and nettles with long sticks. They both wore army boots and backpacks that clanked slightly. Her own sandals rubbed uncomfortably. The canvas bag, packed with sliced bread, milk and loads of bags of sugar, bumped against her leg, making her stumble.

As they descended into the crease of the valley, she felt the cool earthy damp of a stream touch her skin. A bat flitted close to her face. Mosquitoes dithered in her hair. It was dark down here, private, not used to people. The trees grew stunted, their fat, twisted trunks covered with thick pelts of moss. When they startled a couple of deer, she stopped and watched their white tails bobbing off into denser woodland.

She struggled to catch up with the men who walked briskly, talking between themselves without looking back to see where she was. She wondered if they were trying to shake her off. They'd come so far now that without them she was lost.

Her mouth felt dry and she pictured the children wandering round the dark house, calling for her. It wouldn't happen, of course. They only ever woke up in the small hours, but why hadn't she asked David to check on them?

Branches cracked and she glimpsed other people moving through the woods in the same direction, calling softly to each other.

"Jez! Is that you?"

"Nobby! It's this way you pillock."

In truth, she could have turned back, but the buzz of fear and excitement, the sense of determination and common purpose pulled her along. She felt caught up in a surge of energy.

More people flitted between the trees, funnelling towards a clearing. She could smell clay, churned up earth, a sickly reek of shit and wood smoke. Blackened kettles and cooking pots stood on stones beside a central fire pit. People lived here, it seemed, in makeshift shelters, under sheets of canvas and blue plastic pulled over branches and tethered to the ground. Brushing past a tarpaulin she heard a child crying feebly while a man hushed it to sleep.

A group had gathered in the middle of the camp. Silent faces tilted towards a young man with shaved head and glasses who talked softly and chopped the air with his hands.

There were maybe thirty people, she couldn't tell – the mass of bodies grew as more people emerged from the trees to join them every few minutes. She vaguely recognised people, one of their old gardeners, the couple that ran the village shop.

Out in the open, it was surprisingly bright. The deepening indigo sky held a hard, pale moon. There was something else. Another source of light.

Squeezing through the crowd she could make out the edge of the camp. Shivering coils of razor wire lay across the ground, and beyond them, a great wide chalky gash in the valley floor. Smooth and pristine, it threw back the last of midsummer and pulsed in the dying light. The obscenity of it hit her like a body blow. She stepped back, unable to look away. To one side, the stream had been dug out to form a deep gully. Drainage pipes were stacked along the edge, ready to enclose it. Further off stood ranks of yellow diggers and road building machines, then rows of small white caravans.

"First time? Unbelievable, isn't it?" The young woman beside her gave her a pitying look. She was about eighteen with black hair falling in dreadlocks over her matted orange jumper. A fine powder of white dust from the road works gave her a ghostly aura.

"Do you live here?" Jess asked. She thought of the crusties that gathered outside Waitrose drinking cider, dogs on strings.

The girl nodded. The sound of distant music and taunting voices drifted across the wasteland. "Listen," she smiled. "The big protest is right over the other side. The guards and the workers are all busy with that. See, their caravans are dark. Most nights they're inside watching telly."

"Look I've got this." She held out the canvas bag.

"Cheers!" The young woman took it and started pulling out bags of sugar, throwing them to her friends. "Here, take one of these," she flashed a torch onto a pile of tools – wrenches, wire cutters. Everyone was surging forward, grabbing what they needed, then filtering along the side of the razor wire, in the direction of the diggers and caravans.

Jess froze. "I don't think I can do this," she whispered. "Don't worry," said the girl, passing her some heavy wire cutters. "You can come in with me!"

"It's just that I didn't quite mean to," she looked around for bee man and his son thinking they'd be able to explain. "Come on!" The girl was angry, insistent. "You're not just going to stand by and *watch* are you?"

A few people looked round. The girl tugged hard at Jess's arm and they followed the others as they filed along the fence towards a small opening made by propping the wire up with branches. They were close to the diggers and caravans.

"Make it quick," the man at the opening whispered. "We've got ten minutes max. When I whistle, come straight back. That's thirteen, fourteen..." he counted them through. She heard herself panting, heart hammering as they ran towards one of the big yellow machines. The girl clambered up, with wrench and sugar, looking for the fuel cap. "Go for the cables underneath," she ordered Jess. "Just cut through anything".

She scrambled under the black stinking belly of the beast and groped around until she felt a rubber cable cover. Her hands were shaking so much, she couldn't grip the cutters properly. She gritted her teeth and then she felt them slice through. It was blissfully satisfying. She moved on to the next, totally absorbed, as though cutting her way out of a trap into a better place.

She'd just done the third and was looking for a fourth cable when she heard shouts, feet thudding as people scrambled across the white ground, back towards the hole in the fence. For a moment she wondered if she should stay in the dark there hidden, but there were more shouts. She wriggled out and threw herself across the hard ground, the last one to leave.

The man at the hole in the fence waved frantically. "What took you so fucking long?" he whispered harshly. "Didn't you hear us? You put everyone at risk." He carefully lowered the branches, closing the doorway in the razor wire and disappeared into the undergrowth.

As she followed him her sandal caught and she fell, smashing her arm on a rock. An intense burning sensation in her wrist told her she'd done some serious damage, maybe broken it, but she didn't cry out for fear of giving herself away. The sound of the other people pushing through undergrowth receded up the side of the valley.

She lay dead still staring up as the first stars pricked through the night canopy. As well as pain, she felt elation, a thrill of pride, a sense of release from all the things that tied her to this world. The guard dogs' howls subsided. Everyone had left. She felt completely alone in this derelict place.

Gingerly, she picked her way back along the fence towards the camp where she climbed under a tarpaulin, pulled a stinking blanket over her head and fell asleep.

The cold, stony ground woke her at first light. The clear sky tinged delicately with pink. Her wrist throbbed. She made her way back up the valley in the direction of home.

* * *

Stepping into the warm kitchen, the atmosphere felt different. She smelt something welcoming and delicious. Jake, in his chinos and polo shirt, was clattering over the Aga making pancakes.

He stared as she glugged back a pint glass of water. "My *God*, are you alright? Where have you been?"

In the sitting room, Bruno sprawled on the sofa next to the panda faced guy watching Snow White. Tess was curled up on shape shifter's lap while he read her a story.

She looked up and smiled. "Hello Mummy," she said sweetly. "Daddy's looking for you," and turned back to the book.

The crisis she'd created seemed to have cheered everyone up.

She had a bath. Panda man – Jim – turned out to be a first aider. Ever so gently, he cleaned the scratches on her shins and looked at her wrist. Take some ibuprofen he suggested, then go to A and E.

David returned, boggle-eyed with fear and fury. He'd gone to bed thinking she'd fallen asleep with the children. When Bruno came looking for her in the small hours, he'd realised she was missing and raised the alarm. Called the police, called the hospital, driven all around.

As he drove her to A and E, she told him she'd gone out for a walk at dusk and got lost and fallen over. Must have knocked herself out.

"Right! Of course!" he said, slapping his forehead. "Why on earth didn't you tell me you were going out? The children were on their own. The house could have burnt down."

Silence.

"But it didn't," she said.

They waited in A and E for several hours, exchanging the odd word as people shuffled in and out of the airless waiting room.

* * *

It took three more years for the road to be completed. The protesters were evicted from their camp the following winter and some went to prison. It was on the national news. Soon after that, the blasting began. It shook the farmhouse day after day as they dynamited through the down, creating a bleak, white ravine. She could just see it from the edge of their paddock, an incongruous cliff face leering back at her from deep inside the hill.

Then came the swirl of tarmac, snaking south towards the coast, the constant swish of traffic, not loud, but never quiet. The darkness smudged with an orange haze of lights.

She felt a peculiar connection with the road, an intense, private hatred bound her to it. It surprised her that David never questioned her about that night. She could have been anywhere, with anyone! She thought one day she'd tell him, but as time went by it would have seemed odd. And while she never meant it to be a secret, her night in the valley became so embedded in her, such a fragile but reassuring memory of her self, that she couldn't have told it to anyone, for fear of snuffing it out.

Things got easier. She felt happier.

David tired of the Shamanic stuff. It wasn't making enough money. So they started running paintballing in the woods. The sweat lodge served as a base camp. Birthday party packages were popular, with chicken nuggets, oven chips, Cornettos. Business picked up for a bit, but not enough.

They got planning permission for five new houses to be built on the paddock.

A year after the new road opened, they sold up and left the area.

Emma Brooker

Motorway Twitter Poems

Those catseyes aren't really there for the cars: they're stars, shoehorned into rows by some celestial surveyor with an eye for beauty and order.

* * *

Before you sneer at that sweaty sales rep in the middle lane, just remember that he too has a soul and a shortage of cup-holders.

* * *

The hawks hovering gimlet-eyed above the verges aren't looking for mice. They're I-Spy geeks, ticking off the flyovers like trainspotters.

Joe Moran

Diamond Tea

This is not 1990
    this is 2012

land permissions   cooling tower
cloud cover

take it easy with the drugs

"Where's Sean?"

"He'll be laying on his back looking at the stars"

from beyond
    message continuing support

take it easy with the drugs

This is April it is not May

there is an epicness about this
    like a ten pence valentine
yet to be sent

refuge of fire
    out there beyond

the river
> bound homeward

5.15 a.m. record the sound of bird song
> and motorway
from the security of the service area

blanket wrapped couple
> bonfire stare

throw another pallet on

Duracell is breathing fire
> Ringo is asking the same question
over and over and over

Easter
> often cloudy

every Preston Guild it will snow

paint splattered Dolomite

not even 25.6 mg can warm

this is April it is not May

Andrew Taylor

Extract from *Steel Girdered: A Musical in Several Parts*

HER ANATOMY SPLIT OF WEIL'S DISCOURSE

introducing la lady tray ordinaire et plastique open
wide for business fun blasts and cleaning products
buff the glass up in this niche of geographic depression.
Head of Magrot Thatcher 6/6/87 or bust of Adonis,
Lord, who was prohibited from urination despite
funny walking and covert clutching. The rats be
happy, human-free, here where – JULIE! – the place
is fucking firing up your pantry! It burned up down,
the dozy mare.

Do you need hot water and towels for birthing canal?
Nope. Robbie Williams sings crack in the car park
gives local access, a big problem for piggy-wigs,
of many there are on chairs eating enormous iced buns,
looking for the criminal axis of acronyms and continents
or exulting at eggs on plate; here the kids saw Robbie –
who'd have thought it! – and REAL Eastenders and
REAL Iain Sinclair and some REAL nobody writhing in
a backseat penning a tortured-heart rhymer into top
shelf filth about horses.

Blogging, fluffy bear and wrens and wagtails in glass
penetration of natural light; the trees are on the inside
as is newscasting for 14 star loo awards (send that postcard).
Wear a uniform and wsah yuor hnads wiht saop to
smuggle in the vodka in over-sized Alice mugs tripping
through the ornamental maze and advice on yellow food.
Humanely fearless rats endorse the website, quoting the
midwife, "Am I going mad or is this really happening
 with three question marks"

you're getting a picture now, right, of metal rafters, glass up
to them, rats aground pillars of news and plastic chairs with
our heroine here where the A1(M) can meet the M25 and
they make dirty love under the thin light in All Days rooms
among the dried biscuits (survival will be on condiments only
but wait a chopper) this is the erstwhile intro of place famous
faced for anonymous & democratic need to pee: it is the spot
an ordinary woman climbs upon a plastic table from plastic
chair, steadies her heels, looks ahead

and is cleaved in two, a midair cartoon pause before
dropping to the left half a weakly victim of masculogic,
limp hand still outstretched to steady; the other
half a policeperson of language, flapped floorwards
uniformed and truncheoned for the faux-furred.
So: two rubbery skin-images crumpled either side
on quick-clean tiling;
table-topped is the oval
                              egg
                              slight
                              blood
                              warm
                              ish

Jennifer Cooke

* The poem-sequence, *'Steel Girdered Her Musical: In Several Parts'*,
from which this poem is taken is a cross-genre creation, with
music by the composer Adam Robinson.

Cool Sheets

Cool sheets are a welcome relief as the
clock ticks slowly, distant
noise from the motorway soothes,
helps me find a way to sleep.

Andrew Taylor

Twitter poem

Watford Gap grass verge through coffee steam, reassurance of traffic noise, knowing we are an hour away – the beauty of the service station

Andrew Taylor

Afterword

Highways and Byways

A long standing genre of travel writing frames this book on motorways, taking in all manner of roads, railways and waterways, that of 'Highways and Byways'. These works often focus on the byways, the green lanes, branch lines and rivers left behind by modern, faster highway networks, of turnpikes, arterial roads, main rail lines and cross country canals. Indeed motorways themselves in this book appear as byways, once for a short historical moment super highways, now slowing down, with speed limits, coned sections and traffic jams, such than we can at times observe the flourishing verges in slow moving, stopping, traffic even see the car park communities at service stations, swelled by those who have driven off the carriageway just to let the tailback shorten.

Do Twentieth Century British motorways promise to be the byways of a new highway system of European style fast rail links, confirming the wry nostalgia for old classic motorway sections and service stations? Or, apart from a brief moment in the 1960s have British (or is it English?) writers never adopted a Modernist roadster sensibility, happy not to measure up to German or American auto culture, the A47 and Austin Allegro our ironic, jokey versions of the BMW and Route 66. Well, even Route 66 is now a byway, a backroad, to the main Interstate Highway system, sought out mainly by tourists of Americana. Is byway sensibility a central strain of Anglicana? For every streamlined poem like Auden's for the 1936 film documentary *Night Mail*, a work about modern Britain, rattling along with the mainline postal delivery, are there more in the style of Edward Thomas's *Adlestrop* (1917) about the train that makes an unscheduled stop at a Cotswold village station, such that the sights and sounds of nature in summer flood into the carriage? With this rural station now closed, Adlestrop is a poem that has become central to the branchline pastoral of mid Twentieth Century, when its new subtitle might have been 'Marples Must Go'.

Byways are in a sense produced, or activated, by highways, materially and imaginatively. Turnpikes both provided access for tourists to remote regions where country lanes still flourished, and transformed and overtook them. So a standard trope of country writing in Georgian England, found in works by Uvedale Price, Humphry Repton and William Cobbett, is a recollection of a former country lane open to the surrounding countryside, and often embedded in it, as in a hollow way, now smoothed and levelled to form a modern carriage road and cut off from the surrounding landscape. In contrast to this new, fast track, turnpike network, the older routeway would seem more authentic, more socially inclusive, even materially more real, a place not a space; this as writers would imaginatively decelerate, dreaming of a deeper England, sheep rooting among roadside trees, banks of wild flowers, old folks wandering into hospitable parkland, even gypsies camping happily on verges.

A number of contemporary writers also slow down, even scramble on foot across the grain of the motorway system, seeking out a ghostly geography of former routeways, culverted streams, stretches of former turnpike, old footpaths and towpaths. For some this is a matter of critique, not retreat; a radical reverie, gaining access to half hidden modern networks of power, as the ghostly hero does in Patrick Keiller's 2010 film *Robinson in Ruins*, wandering down old coach roads and bridleways to find by the fields a grid of oil pipelines and satellite communication, the hard military state within the softer contours of the Oxfordshire countryside. For others, the stroll down byways appears more conventional, a form of peripheral vision now codifying into a picturesque vista. Once off the beaten track, so called edgelands are now where the literary action is, crowded with a varied cast of deep topographers, new nature writers, literary cartographers and psychogeographers. With their picturesque mix of technical detritus and flourishing wildlife, do edgelands seem now more central than peripheral to the national geographical imagination, liminal zones passing into landscape scenery? Contributors to this book mostly resist this inclination, tracing the British motorway through the matrix of highway and byway.

In 2011 Trowell, a village on the edge of Nottingham, now nationally known for naming a service station on the M1, celebrated the 60th anniversary of the brief moment in 1951 when it was commemorated as the official Festival Village for the Festival of Britain. It was chosen by the Labour Adminstration because it was not a conventional picturesque village, for it had no village green or pub, indeed Trowell was a largely industrial village whose livelihood was based on the ironworks, but perhaps could demonstrate that post-war modernity should be progress to a brighter and better future. The village was also estimated to be the geographical centre of England (a reminder of how anglocentric definitions of Britain can be) if located by the Festival programme nearly a hundred miles to the south of Nottinghamshire in Northamptonshire. Trowell's moment of modernity as a model industrial village, in the rail and canal corridor of the Erewash Valley, was brief, if anyone actually seriously believed the promotional hype. It came to an end with another moment of modernity in the motorway age when the northern section of the M1 sliced through the village and a service station opened in 1966 to the north of the village on former farmland. As Peter Merriman notes in his definitive cultural geography of the M1, the book *Driving Spaces* (2007) the exterior was standard for Mecca service stations but the interior made a gesture to local heritage, if of a rustic kind, with a Robin Hood theme, including 'Sheriff's Restaurant' and a replica of an ancient landmark in Sherwood Forest, the Major Oak. With its ironworks closed and the recently widened motorway thundering by, Trowell is not one of those dead end, severed villages which byway connoisseurs have sought out over the centuries, it is an edgeland of a sort, an expanding, largely residential suburb of Nottingham.

Stephen Daniels

Contributors' Index:

Alsop, John: p29, p30, p31, p32, p33, p106, p116, p117, p173.
Andrews, Malcolm: p77, p127, p128, p173.
Brooker, Emma: p154, p173.
Calvert, John: p79, p173.
Chell, Edward: Title page; as co-editor, p16, p42, p72, p127, p173.
Cooke, Jennifer: p161, p173.
Corkish, Alan: Title page; as editor, p97, p174.
Cowie, Elizabeth: p46, p99, p174.
Crewe, Sarah: p50, p174.
Daniels, Stephen: p167, p174.
Davies, John: p14, p24, p111, p175.
Keaton, Angela: p97, p175.
Kelder, Cralan: p49, p175.
Lawrence, David: p93, p98, p100, p175.
McCabe, Chris: p39, p175.
Moran, Joe: p15, p51, p101, p113, p119, p121, p127, p128, p176.
Mutch, Hazel: p37, p176.
Sinclair, Iain: p15, p22, p35, p49, p84, p94, p176.
Taylor, Andrew: Title page; as co-editor, p13, p27, p129, p133, p134, p159, p162, p176.
Webb, Mike: p15, p98, p176.

Index of Names:

Andre, Carl: p41, p46, p125.
Armitage, Simon: p84, p94, p113.
Auden, W.H.: p165.
Augé, Marc: p15, p59, p60, p64, p73, p77, p78.
Austen, Jane: p57, p125, p128.
Ballard, J.G.: p15, p119, p126.
Banham, Reyner: p61, p78.
Barnard, Clio: p41, p44, p45, p46, p99.

Barnett, Cliff: p105.
Barthes, Roland: p53, p55, p56, p59, p74, p77, p78, p101.
Benjamin, Walter: p131.
Berger, John: p82, p94.
Betjeman, John: p127.
Bowen, Miranda: p94.
Bowie, David: p90.
Bremner, Billy: p32.
Britton, Dave: p33.
Britton, John: p175.
Brontë, Emily: p127.
Brooks-Gordon, Belinda: p94.
Brown, Lancelot (Capability): p122, p125.
Buren, Daniel: p131.
Burke, Edmund: p128.
Calvert, Margaret: p133.
Cave, Peter L.: p94.
Cobbett, William: p166.
Cocker, Emma: p45, p46.
Cortázar, Julio: p15.
Criswell, Henry: p124.
Cross, Andrew: p123.
Dagion, John W.: p94.
Defoe, Daniel: p30.
Dimendberg, Edward: p61, p78.
Drake, James: p125.
Duchamp, Marcel: p162.
Dunlop, Carol: p15.
Echo and the Bunnymen: p132.
Edensor, Tim: p23.
Eliot, T.S.: p23.
Endfield, C. Raker: p94.
Farley, Paul: p15, p122, p127.
Finney, Albert: p87, p94.
Fletcher, David: p116.
Friedlander, Lee: p61.
Furie, Sidney J.: p91.

Gaiger, J: p128.
Gilpin, William: p125.
Godwin, Fay: p122, p127.
Gormley, Antony: p34.
Gursky, Andreas: p123.
Hallam, Paul: p94.
Hazlitt, William: p128.
Heseltine, Michael: p114.
Hopper, Edward: p87, p94.
Hornsey, Richard: p94.
Hurst, Charles: p22, p23.
Huskisson, William: p23.
Inman, Jeff: p94.
It's Immaterial: p133.
Joy Division: p132.
Keiller, Patrick: p30, p123, p166.
Kieran and Guy: p19, p24.
Kinneir, Jock: p133.
Kraftwerk: p90.
Lennon, John: p117.
Long, Richard: p126.
Lorraine, Claude: p124.
Lunan, Mary: p94.
Macfarlane, R.: p128.
Manning, Bernard: p33.
Marples, Ernest: p114.
Marshall, William: p76, p77.
Merriman, Peter: p167.
Meyerowitz, Joel: p61.
Miller, Graeme: p15.
Mitchell, Cari: p94.
Moorcock, Michael: p32.
Morse, Margaret: p46.
Mort, Frank: p94.
Moses, Robert: p124.
Nietzsche, Friedrich: p46.
Orwell, George: p41.

Osborne, Peter D: p61, p62, p78.
Pankhurst, Emmeline: p22.
Panse, S.: p127.
Papadimitriou, Nick: p22.
Peck, Ron: p87, p94.
Petit, Chris: p23, p30, p32, p33, p34.
Prescott, John: p32, p166.
Price, Uvedale : p166.
Ray, Nicholas: p32.
Repton, Humphry: p166.
Rouch, Jean: p45.
Robinson, Adam: p50
Sandby, Paul: p123, p124.
Shoard, Marion: p126, p127, p128.
Shuttleworth, John: p115.
Simmel, George: p84, p94.
Smith, Phil: p21, p22.
Sokurov, Alexandr: p127.
Solnit, Rebecca: p23.
Solà-Morales Rubió, Ignassi de: p121, 127.
Stiles, Nobby: p32.
Sutcliffe, Peter: p91.
Swindells, Kerri: p94.
Symmons-Roberts, Michael: p15, p122, p127.
Thatcher, Margaret: p14, p49, p90, p115, p116.
Thomas, Edward: p165.
Van Gogh, Vincent: p31.
Vermuyden, Cornelius: p21,
Wade, George (General): p123.
Wilde, Oscar: p88.
Williams, Owen: p124.
Wood, Harrison C.: p128.
Wood, Jeremy: p94.
Wordsworth, William: p31, p127.
Zachmann, Patrick: p61, p62.

In the Company of Ghosts; contributors' Biographies:

Prof. Will Alsop is one of the UK's most prominent, award-winning architects, guided by the principle that architecture is both a vehicle and symbol of social change and renewal. Alsop follows a parallel path as an artist; his stance is that art and architecture are inseparable disciplines. He is founder of ALL Design, Professor at Vienna's Technical University and continues to hold many academic posts around the world.

Malcolm Andrews is Emeritus Professor at the University of Kent. He is editor of the journal The Dickensian, and author of a number of books on Dickens and on landscape in art and literature, including *The Search for the Picturesque* (Scolar Press, 1989) and *Landscape and Western Art* (Oxford, 1999). His book *Dickens and Laughter* is due to be published in 2013.

Emma Brooker studied English at Cambridge University and Creative Writing at UEA. She lives in London and teaches at London South Bank University.

John Calvert is a poet, musician and performer based in Manchester. His work has been widely published and performed in various venues. He is at present compiling a collection of his work.

Edward Chell is Senior Lecturer in Fine Art, UCA, Canterbury. An RCA graduate, recent solo shows include *Viewing Stations* (Tank Gallery, London) and *Gran Tourismo*, Cumbria (supported by Grizedale Arts) both in 2011. *Ten Steps to Heaven*, an Arts Council supported permanent installation commissioned by the Swedenborg Society, London, was part of *Fourteen Artists Interventions* in 2010 with *In Conversation* (with Amy Halliday) published by them in 2011. He has been awarded an AHRC fellowship for his 'Soft Estate' project.

Jennifer Cooke is a London-based poet. Her forthcoming collection is entitled _*not suitable for domestic sublimation_. She's Lecturer in English at Loughborough University and author of _Legacies of Plague in Literature, Theory and Film (2009)_, as well as articles on modernism, psychoanalysis, Hélène Cixous and contemporary poetry.

Alan Corkish is an editor, academic, literary-reviewer and widely published author from Liverpool UK, co-founder with Dr Andrew Taylor of *erbacce* and erbacce-press. His initial Hons Degree is from Liverpool University and he also holds an MA from Lancaster and an MSc from Keele; over 500 of his poems and short stories have been published in books and journals world-wide... in a previous life he was (is) a time-served stone-mason, a docker, a stoker on a steam-ship, farm-hand and street-sweeper. Currently he works part-time in the NHS as a psychotherapist.

Elizabeth Cowie is Professor of Film Studies at the University of Kent, Canterbury. Her books include *Representing the Woman: Cinema and Psychoanalysis* (Macmillan, 1997) and *Recording Reality, Desiring the Real* (Minnesota University Press, 2011). She has written on film noir, on the horror of the horror film, and the cinematic dream-work.

Sarah Crewe is 30 and from the Port of Liverpool. Her chapbook, *Aqua Rosa*, was published by erbacce press in April 2012. Her work has also appeared at *Otoliths, 3:AM, The Camel Saloon, streetcake* and *erbacce* magazine. Her favourite motorway route is M62-M6-M5-A38 and turning left at Indian Queens.

Stephen Daniels As a nine year old Stephen remembers being taken on a Sunday drive on the newly opened M1 in the family Morris 8, or does he imagine it from looking at newsreels of the time? He is now Professor of Cultural Geography at the University of Nottingham and Director of the AHRC programme in Landscape and Environment. He is author and co-author of many works on the history of landscape and the geographical imagination, including books on Humphry Repton and Paul Sandby. He is currently researching a book on the Nineteenth Century topographical publisher John Britton and for the

National Trust installing an Eighteenth Century style magic lantern show in a converted Norfolk barn.

John Davies is a Church of England vicar in deeply rural West Devon. Born and raised by the banks of the River Mersey, John's writing and thinking are keenly influenced by that city's great poets (not least Ken Dodd, Ian McCulloch, G.M. Hopkins, and the people you meet at bus stops everyday). Writer, broadcaster and preacher on the subject of finding heaven in the ordinary, John, a keen walker, does his thinking on his feet. The diary of his 2007 TransPennine journey, *Walking the M62* is published by Lulu Press.

Angela Keaton was born in Cheshire UK. She was educated in North West England and in Brussels. Traces of the influences, of Oulipo, the Language Poets and Zen can be found in her writing but she makes of them something that differs from them and is distinctly her own. Her work has appeared in several literary journals and anthologies and she has had three chap-books of poems published by erbacce-press.

Cralan Kelder was born in 1970, growing up in California and The Netherlands. Publications include: *Big Deal Rimbaud* (smallMinded 2011), *Give Some Word* (Shearsman 2010), *City Boy* (Longhouse 2007), and *Lemon Red* (Coracle 2005). He lives in Amsterdam with the evolutionary biologist Toby Kiers and their children, where they currently reside *sans* automobile, using a contraption called a *bakfiets* instead.

Dr. David Lawrence is a writer and cultural archaeologist specialising in places where people, architecture and movement meet such as motorway service areas and underground stations. He is the author of *Food on the Move: the extraordinary world of the motorway service area*, and a regular contributor to radio, television and related media.

Chris McCabe was born in Liverpool in 1977. His published books are *The Hutton Inquiry* (Salt, 2005), *Zeppelins* (Salt, 2008) and a play *Shad Thames, Broken Wharf* (Penned in the Margins 2010). He has also recorded a CD with The Poetry Archive. His third full collection, *THE RESTRUCTURE*, was published in April 2012.

Joe Moran is a writer and academic, based at Liverpool John Moores University. His most recent books are *Queuing for Beginners* (2007), a cultural history of daily habits since the war, and *On Roads: A Hidden History* (2009). He is currently writing a history of watching television. He writes for the *Guardian*, the *Financial Times* and other publications.

Hazel Mutch has lived in various northern towns and seems to have settled in Ormskirk, Lancashire, where she lives with her daughter. She makes her living mentoring students, and from feltmaking and sometimes painting. She has an MA in Creative Writing from Edge Hill University, which has generated a fascination with poetics.

Iain Sinclair lives in East London. After walking much of the local terrain, he took to motorway fringes and the footprints of fleeing poets. His most recent publication is *Ghost Milk: Calling Time on the Grand Project*. A film, *Swandown*, directed by Andrew Kötting, documents a voyage he made, by swan pedalo, from Hastings to the Olympic site in the Lower Lea Valley.

Andrew Taylor is a Liverpool poet and co-founder of *erbacce* and erbacce-press. His poems have been widely published on-line and in print. After several pamphlets, his first full collection of poetry is forthcoming from Shearsman. He has a PhD in poetry and poetics and currently teaches creative writing at Edge Hill University.

Michael Webb gained a distinction in his Foundation Degree. For the next three years Michael studied at Nottingham Trent University where he obtained a degree in Graphic Design. He currently works for a sign company in the North West.